Passive Inc

For 2020

A Step by Step Guide to Easy Passive Income Ideas For 2020 and Beyond

Author: Ralf Percy

Table of Contents

Book Description:

Are you ready to invest your money into creating passive income streams that inflate your monthly income? These are some of the hottest, proven methods that you can start with, today.

You're not going to get rich earning a salary. You need to take those savings and make money from money. But how? It can be harrowing and risky to invest in new income streams for the first time. The chance that you will lose money is high. That's why you need a guide just like this one.

In *Passive Income Ideas for 2019*, I detail some of the most lucrative methods of earning additional income available for the modern investor. I take a candid, unfiltered look at opportunities in social media, drop shipping, affiliate marketing and renting. There is real money to be made here!

In this ideas-guide you'll learn:

- Why passive income will get you where you want to go
- How drop-shipping works and how to get started selling
- What affiliate marketing is and how to make money this way
- How to invest as someone interested in passive income
- How to leverage social media for passive income generation
- About renting, website flipping, selling eBooks and being a creative

The sky is the limit when you're no longer a slave to your monthly paycheck. You'll lose some. And you'll win some too. After a while, you'll just keep winning. That's when your life changes.

Discover how to seriously create passive income streams that will free you from your current job. It's easier than you think, and all it takes is commitment and a sharp mind!

Learn how to get started with passive income in this guide.

Buy the guide, and start earning!

Introduction

Are you struggling to make money? Do you feel like you are spending most of your time, yet you have nothing to show for it? Do you admire those millionaires and billionaires on TV and wonder how they do it? If the answer is yes, then you might want to ask yourself how you can get out of your own way and start making more money. The answer is to that is also simple; you are not doing everything you can to make more money. You may wonder how that is if you are spending all your waking hours working. The answer is you do not have a PASSIVE INCOME stream. For years, rich people have understood that it's not how much work you do that makes you rich, that it is the quality of work that you do. You can spend all day working hard but still get paid minimum wages for it. There is also the danger of getting fired abruptly which makes you lose everything if you were not prepared.

Rich people understand that the money they have should work for them. They put their money in avenues that make them more money. They, however, do not sit down and enjoy their wealth. They keep putting their money in avenues that keep making a profit. They ensure that they make money even when they are not involved in said investments. This is what separates the rich and the poor.

If you have a little money and a lot of patience, then this is the book for you. Active income is the money you receive in your bank account that you earn from a job you do. It is what most people rely on to survive. For years, people have been urged to save money before they spend the rest. Even if your bills take up a huge percentage of your earnings, you can still save something. If you can't save anything, then that tells you that you are living beyond your means.

Don't put all of your money in a bank and assume that it is safe there. It might be safe, but it is not doing anything to safeguard your future. That money is what you should take out and invest in passive income generating ventures. Passive income is that which you earn even when you are not working for it. You get money from doing nothing basically. To earn a passive income, the bulk of the work is done upfront, and then the return will trickle in for as long as the investment remains active. The money you receive monthly may not be significant, but if you save it for a long time, together with compound interest, you will see the difference. You have to be patient before you see some tangible impact of your impact, but once it starts, it never stops.

There are many ways to make passive income and the returns from each vary. The more the return, the more you may have to get involved. I'm not saying you have to spend all your time on it. I'm saying you have to be involved. You may need to put in a little time to make the investment earn more, but it can still run without it. If you hate doing work, this is not for you. This is because passive income is not a get rich quick scheme. The work may be demanding, but the results make it all worthwhile.

The fact that passive income is a sure way of making extra money doesn't mean that the field remains rigid. You will constantly have to learn what is changing in the industry could make a world of difference in your returns in the long run. Look at trends and what people are looking for, but you still need to add our personality to it to make it even better.

Why the Need for Passive Income?

Even though we keep saying that passive income is money we don't have to work for, we have to remember that we traded that money for time sometime in the past. Passive income is a direct time of continuous efforts over some time. Even if you still earn from something you created ten years ago, there is no shame in telling that to people. There would be nothing unethical here especially if you did some work that is paying off years later.

- You will be free to pursue other things instead of chasing after money. You may still have your active income, but your days will be freer for you to rest and spend time with family instead of taking a second job to meet your basic requirements. Some people earn a lot of passive income that they can leave jobs they hate to pursue what they are passionate about. They are sorted even if their passions don't pay them right away.

- You will be able to plan for the future with the extra money. The greatest fear among working people is what will happen if they retired, and they are more worried if they are unable to put something aside for retirement when they can no longer work. Passive income eliminates that from your mind because as you work for your day to day expenses, your investments are working for your retirement.

- If you are trying to build multiple passive income streams, you can do so as opposed to traditional jobs here you are limited to a desk in a particular place. The internet becomes your workplace as you can communicate with clients and potential customers without leaving your home.

- With passive income, there is nowhere else to go but up if you play your cards right. This doesn't include risky investments. It includes the streams of passive income that have worked for many years. Even if the return starts out small, there is steady growth over a period of time as long as people are still interested in what you are selling. This will also happen if you keep marketing yourself and establishing yourself as an authority on a certain subject matter.

- Passive income is the foundation for wealth in the long run. The discipline it takes to work on something other than the one you have to do makes you appreciate the money you make. You may be a business owner that makes a lot of money. Until you make your money work for you aka investing, you are still not wealthy.

- Passive income saves you the most precious commodity that you can't gain back once lost–time. If you can exchange the time, you spend chasing money to pay bills and survive then you have won in life. As John Wooden so elegantly stated, "Don't let making a living prevent you from making a life."

Chapter 1
Dropshipping

The best time to plant a tree was 20 years ago. The second-best time to plant a tree is today.

Chinese Proverb

Drop shipping has recently gained traction in the passive income space. It has especially been very profitable because of people's love for online shopping. Here, you as the seller have a website, but you don't necessarily own the product you are selling. It is like a brokerage between the customer and a third-party seller. You never see the product because the product is directly shipped from the third-party seller to the client. The third party here is a wholesaler or a manufacturer. You as a drop shipper never handle the inventory, therefore, reducing the need for a physical location as with usual retailers.

How Does Drop Shipping Work?

The first thing to notice is that Drop shipping is a service that is provided to a customer by a person behind a computer. The manufacturer produces items for sale but doesn't sell directly to the final consumer. This is because it rarely makes any financial sense to sell an item at a time if they deal with millions of products at a go. They offer their products at a lower price in bulk and have little to no purchase requirements, making it convenient for retailers with a lot of capital and wholesalers to buy directly from them. The wholesaler buys from the manufacturer and then raise the cost a little higher to make a profit. They also sell most of their products in bulk as opposed to a single item. The end consumer, therefore, can purchase items whatever the number from a retailer. The retailer buys from a wholesaler and raises the cost even higher to cater to their profit margins. These are the three groups of people that are available in a supply chain, and therefore as a drop shipper, you are a retailer. The drop shipping model is not visible to the end consumer at all. You as the drop shipper can purchase your products from any of the three groups even if you are a retailer. As long as any of them is willing to ship their products to your end user, they are "drop shipping" for you.

Step 1: Order Placement by Customer

A customer surfs through your niche website and finds a product that they want to buy. You as the merchant gets a message informing you of the purchase. Simultaneously, the customer receives a confirmation message of the purchase. The order is automatically generated by the software and sent via email to both parties. The payment is also automatically processed by a payment software, and confirmations are made to both parties.

Step 2: Order placement to the supplier

The order confirmation message is sent to the supplier so that they can process and ship the order to the customer. The supplier debits the total cost of the item from the merchant's account. Their price will be lower than what is charged by the merchant. The price will include order processing fees, shipping fees and the cost of the item. It is therefore up to the merchant to have considered this when they charged the consumer.

Step 3: Order Dispatch from the supplier warehouse

The supplier boxes and ships the item to customer depending on how fast their service is. All this should be included when marketing to the customer. The merchant's logo, address, and contact number are what shall appear on the box and not that of the supplier. Upon shipping, an alert is sent to the merchant along with a tracking number for the order. They also send an invoice for accounting purposes to the merchant.

Step 4: The merchant informs the customer about the shipment

An email alert is sent to the customer with the order tracking information by the merchant through the store's software. The order is complete at this point.

How to Find Suppliers to Work with

As I said before, the difference between success and failure in drop shipping is a reliable supplier. The end user doesn't know that there is a third party involved in the sale. Therefore you will be the one responsible if the item is not shipped, is damaged or of poor quality. Consequently, one needs to work with a supplier that will work well with your business model. You will also need to differentiate between legitimate wholesalers from posers and scammers. How can you separate the fake from the true wholesalers you may ask?

- They want you to pay them a monthly fee instead of charging you for the items you order from them. A legitimate supplier may charge a processing fee, but it is a reasonable amount, and they explain what they are charging you for so you know beforehand. Legitimate fees you will encounter are order processing fees that are added to each order you make. They will also have a minimum amount of goods you buy as your first purchase to weed out buyers from window shoppers. Instead of buying the items, you can advance them the total amount for an order that will go into your merchant account.

- If they are claiming to be wholesalers and yet they are selling directly to customers. This makes the prices go way up as they want to make as much money as they do if they sell directly to the client. That will eat into your profit margins.

There are many ways in which a merchant can find wholesale suppliers to work with.

1. Getting in touch with manufacturers

If you know the products you want to sell, looking for manufacturers to work with is not hard. All you have to do is finding out from them a list of their distributors. From then you can look for the one that does drop shipping and asks for requirements to set up an account with them.

2. Make use of the internet

The internet is full of information as everyone is advertising online. Depending on your niche, many people offer the service you need. Be careful as you can also encounter scammers. Don't just settle for the first suppliers that you see on the top page. Go deeper into the search engines as many good wholesalers may be hidden in the result searches. Look at the offers as opposed to the design of their websites. Don't give up on the first try and don't expect to get a good wholesaler immediately.

3. Scout, your competitor's supplier

Finding a wholesaler is hard and what better way to get one than good old fashion espionage. You can order from your competitor. You can call the number on the return address which is more likely to be the supplier.

4. Trade fairs and shows

Many manufacturers go to trade fairs where they network with potential retailers. The trade fairs are arranged according to the products, and you can easily pinpoint manufacturers in your niche. Some are free, and others have an attendance fee. Take advantage of many manufacturers in the same place.

5. Directories

There are many directories in the market that you can look for suppliers in your niche. They include SaleHoo, Doba, Wholesale Central and so on.

Attributes of a Good Supplier

- Professionalism and experience

If you are new at drop shipping, a professional representative will be able to talk you through the process and assure you along the way. They can also be able to answer your questions on any topic you may have.

- Around the clock support

Suppliers that answer the client's questions swiftly inspire confidence with the client.

- Tech-savvy organization

Because drop shipping is done from all corners of the globe, technology is the only thing that is unifying every player in the game. Orders and payments have to be done swiftly and securely through state-of-the-art software to improve customer experience. At the bare minimum, they should have email connectivity.

- Good location

If you are a drop shipper, you may want to look for a supplier that is close to almost all your clients to improve the delivery time while reducing shipping costs.

- Efficiency

A good supplier cares about your customer satisfaction which will guarantee you a repeat customer. They will provide good quality products and handle the shipping process with care and urgency.

How to Pick the Right Product for Dropshipping

Drop shipping is an online business, and the best way to know what people want is to search on the Internet. With SEO, it is easy to understand what people are looking to buy online through keyword searches. You can also see what people in your geographic location, what to buy and then what is in during a particular season. Remember that drop shipping is not a static business and those that evolve make the most money.

Consider the price at which the supplier is offering. The price at which you offer the customer should be reasonable; otherwise, you will need to offer phone support for assurance. The recommended price range for most online customers is $50-$200. Sell a product with a MAP (minimum advertised price) pricing so that there isn't much difference in prices between you and the competition.

Look at the scalability and longevity of your business. Your product should be able to stand the test of time and the tides of trends. Consider how you can market the product to potential customers. Sell things that go together so that the customer doesn't click away from your website.

Sell items that do not change with time or perishable goods.

Look at what customers need to find the perfect items to sell. If something can be bought at a local store, then it is not worth the time. Avoid bigger and fragile products as they are expensive to ship and may break down during shipping. Also, avoid items that could be faulty when the customer tests it out. You want to run a business without returns and complaints to keep getting positive reviews.

Advantages of Dropshipping

1. Starting capital is small compared to having a physical location

All a merchant requires is a website to display the products they are selling. They do not need to buy any inventory or storage space to keep it. This reduces the starting capital to a bare minimum. The Dropshipping model ensures that you make a sale first before buying it from the supplier and even then, the burden of packaging and shipping lies with the third party. The cost of running the business is also low as there is no physical store to run. Overhead expenses like rent, employees' salaries, office supplies, and licenses are not something a drop shipper has to worry about. They only need a computer, reliable internet connection and a website to do their business which is monthly services and can be accessed at a low cost

2. It is an easy business to start

Compared to many businesses today, starting a Drop shipping business can be easy. Everything you need to know about running an online business can be accessed online. You can also keep improving your marketing skill after starting the business as there is nothing for you to lose. Compared to business people with an inventory, you don't need to worry about stock taking, office management. As you will not be handling any inventory, the stress of replacing finished products, packing and shipping orders to clients or getting a warehouse is not yours. Making sure orders get to the clients and dealing with returns is also someone else's business.

3. You are not bound to any location

You can start a Drop shipping business anywhere in the world as long as you have a laptop and a strong internet connection. With the availability of large e-commerce stores that can help you connect with manufacturers directly, you can do business with anyone in the world today. Payments can also be made online without the merchant, customer and the manufacturer ever meeting face to face. All you need is trust and reliability coupled with connectivity to the internet.

4. You can sell a wide range of items

A standard retailer worries about space and cost of purchasing inventory when deciding what they want to sell. This is not the case with drop shippers. All they need to do is check if the client has the product in stock and then they put it up on the website for sale. A drop shipper can have different categories and selections for different customers as long as the third party can supply it to the customer.

5. It takes a short time for the new business to scale upward

The problem standard retail model is that with more customers, the processing of orders increases and thus the need to hire more stuff. This burden is absent in this case as, despite the increase in orders, it's the supplier that deals with packaging and shipping. This doesn't affect the merchant in any way except maybe making payments more frequently which hardly seems like a con. The other work that may increase maybe in customer care but that can be solved with one employee or two.

Disadvantages of Dropshipping

1. Some niches have low-profit margins

Depending on the niche that you choose to go into, there is the possibility of making a little profit per item. In the beginning, the merchant may under-price to get traffic to the website. He or she will have to sell a lot of products so that they can make more money in the long run which can take a while to happen. There is also a lot of competition online, and the customers will end up picking the website that offers the lowest price.

2. You have to choose the right supplier

Unless you have the utmost trust that your supplier will deliver the products to the customers at the right time and in the right condition, your business is bound to fail. Standard retailers don't face this problem as they can assure quality control in their inventory and shipping process. You will, therefore, need to experiment until you get the right partner. Customer complaints will most definitely be directed towards you despite the mishap not being our fault. Ensure you communicate with your suppliers constantly to improve the shipping process and reduce complaints.

3. The challenges of dealing with multiple suppliers

As a drop shipper, it isn't uncommon to deal with many suppliers at the same time. Some may be dependable, but some may not, and the customer may buy items that come from different suppliers. First, there may be significant differences in shipping costs that may not make sense to the customer. Computing different shipping charges from different suppliers may be hard because the cost may be too much for a customer to handle. You may, therefore, have to standardize the charges which may come from your pocket.

Despite being an easy way to make passive income, Drop shipping requires a lot of dedication and hard work. It is not a get rich quick scheme. These challenges can be overcome if the merchant uses different strategies from everyone else.

Chapter 2
Affiliate Marketing

Residual income is passive income that comes in every month whether you show up or not. It's when you no longer get paid on your personal efforts alone, but you get paid on the efforts of hundreds or even thousands of others and your money! It's one of the keys to financial freedom and time freedom.

-Steve Fisher

Affiliate marketing is the perfect way to make extra money. With affiliate marketing, you earn money by putting your audience onto a company's product, and if they end up buying, you earn a commission. You are like a middle man between a consumer and a company. You will need to understand the four players in the entire affiliate marketing process.

- The product creator or the seller is the person that owns a certain brand and could benefit from people buying their product.

- An affiliate network is a program that links product creators to interests affiliate marketers. Even though the product creator can get affiliate marketers on their own, it is safer for the affiliate marketer to use an affiliate link. They can track their earnings and ensure they are paid on time through a legitimate affiliate network.

- An affiliate marketer is a person that takes advantage of an offer to market products from a product creator to get people to but their product in exchange for a percentage of the sale. They are in charge of aggressive marketing as they earn from what they sell. A super affiliate is someone who is driving up the sales of the product they promote.

- The end consumer who buys the product promoted by the affiliate marketer.

In affiliate marketing, you can make money as both a product creator or as an affiliate marketer.

4 Steps to Become a Product Creator

A product creator can be known by many names. They include seller, merchant, a brand, vendor or retailer. As a seller, you make a product and have an affiliate marker sell it for you.

Step 1: Look for a great product idea

As a seller, don't jump into creating a product without thinking the idea through. Think of a product that many people need in their life and solves a certain problem they have. Take time to perfect the idea to come up with a product people are willing to buy. Look into products in popular niches that people are searching for online. Instead of coming up with an idea from thin air, consider looking at what already exists in the market and improve on it. Don't be rigid when it comes to ideas; change your mind depending on what you learn about a certain niche. It is always better to look for inspiration from things that you are already interested in or knowledgeable about. This saves you time as you know the important basics that you will need to build upon.

Step 2: Research to see if people like the idea and if there is a need it fills

After getting the idea that you want to pursue, carry out market research to see if people would buy. The market is the true test of a successful product, and people would buy what they want as opposed to what you are selling to them. You can use available research tools like Buzzsumo to know what people are currently into. Once you are sure, you can test the market by asking people if they would buy the product. If so, let them preorder so that you can see if they would spend money on your product.

Step 3: Make the product

There are many resources online that tell you exactly how to create great digital products. Whether its online courses and webinars, instructional eBooks or podcasts; follow instructions from people who are knowledgeable in each field make a useful product that solves a problem. Remember to deliver the finished product to the buyers that pre-ordered and get some feedback on it. Create a website that allows people to learn more about your product and buy it.

Step 4: Join an affiliate network or look for affiliate marketers to market your product

It's finally time to bring in affiliates on board. You can join an affiliate network and connect to affiliates. One thing you have to keep in mind is that the most useful affiliates are the ones already in your niche. They already have an audience that wants to buy products like yours, and this can translate into sales for your product. So how can you get affiliate marketers in your niche? Search online for pop up sites that are in the same niche as you and pitch to them a collaboration.

A good thing to remember is that if your product goes deep in a certain niche, the easier it will be to get fellow merchants to support you. A proposal on a prospective partnership should detail how both of you will benefit in the long run. For you get people who are willing to market your product, you have to give them a good deal on the commission. If you offer commissions between 45-60%, then more people will be willing to come on board. The reason big companies offer low commissions is that they have many affiliate marketers and their product is easy to market as people already know the product. Since your product is new, you will not get the same result if you are stingy with pay-outs. They are even more likely to work harder to bring in customers as they are motivated. Look for YouTube channels in the same niche and tell them about your product and make them an offer.

If you have a website already, start writing blog posts telling people about your product and mention that you would also like affiliate marketers to come on board. Growing an email list and sharing on your social media platforms can also attract some affiliate marketers.

4 Ways to Make Money as an Affiliate Marketer

1. Join an Affiliate network

Joining an affiliate program enables you to see products that are on sale and need affiliate marketing. When you choose an affiliate program, for example, Amazon Associates, you can get a sharable affiliate link that you can share with your audience that they can click to buy. That is the link that identifies you and is the one you will use in all your marketing strategies.

2. Review products online

People lie to see what they are buying and what better way to do that than watching someone testing it for them. By showing people how good the product is, you will capture their attention such that when you give them a call to action to buy the product, they will do just that. Ensure you give honest reviews and sell only products you are sure about. That is the only way you will become an authority in your niche. I think by now you know you have to pick a niche and stick to it. You can write your review on a website or make a video review and post on YouTube. A clever way to make more money is to do multiple reviews in one and put all the affiliate links in the post for people to choose what they like best. On your website, you can have links to products you have tried, tested and loved. They can be products, resources or other items you feel confident about.

3. Comparing products

This is a good way to get people to buy using your link as there are many similar products that people find it hard to choose from. If a person stumbles upon your post, they will most likely buy because they were searching for the best of the two or three products. The comparison has to offer in-depth insight into both products and consider giving them an honest recommendation.

4. E-mail marketing

This is a popular marketing strategy that has earned some affiliate marketers 6 figure commissions. For any affiliate marketer, a community of people that respect and trust your opinion is vital as they are likely to be your customers when you suggest a product. The bigger your email list the more leverage you have when you have a product to promote. But how can you build an email list that you can convert into a loyal customer base? First, you will need software that creates for you a landing page and an automated response email marketing tool.

Remember that people will subscribe to your email list if you offer them something that they need. It shouldn't always be about selling something to them but rather appreciate them by giving them lead magnets. A lead magnet is a tool used by affiliate marketers to attract people to sign up for an email list. They include free courses, planners and budgeting tools, eBooks pretty much anything you can think of that people would want so that they keep looking out for more of it. A good lead magnet is free, simple to understand, straight to the point, related to the website niche and most importantly it should provide value to the customer. When you create a lead magnet, get its special URL and upload it to an accessible site. A tip here is to cleverly add your affiliate links in your lead magnet to maximize profits.

Remember we talked about landing pages earlier, but it has other names too. It is also called a capture, squeeze or lead page. Its main aim is to attract the visitor and make him, or she sign up with their email. Whatever the software or design you use, you then connect the landing page with your email collecting tool.

Automation is the heart and soul of passive income and in affiliate marketing in particular. You don't need to be constantly typing and updating content for your email list when you can schedule content and still be effective in other areas. In email marketing, get an autoresponder that follows up with a series of emails that add value to your subscribers and subtly reminds them of what you are selling. Don't spam peoples mail as they will surely unsubscribe. Keep them interested with more free stuff, and use language then makes them feel like your friend and not a customer.

Advantages of Affiliate Marketing

1. Low overhead and cheap to start

Whether you decide to become a product creator or an affiliate marketer, you only need a computer, a website or YouTube channel and internet connection. The only payment you will make as for hosting the website.

2. Products are digital

Digital products are cheap to create because they don't occupy space in a warehouse, and they don't require shipping to reach the consumer. In case someone is an affiliate marketer, they do not need to create any product at all, therefore, saving themselves some time.

3. It's flexible

Compared to other businesses and jobs, there is no designated time or place that one should be at to succeed. As long as you have a steady internet connection and are dedicated, you shall succeed. There is also no limit to the number of affiliate products you can market at the same time. Automation means that you can earn even when you are offline.

4. Earning potential

As I stated before, people are making 6-7 figure incomes by promoting products online. Depending on your strategies towards earning a passive income, nothing is stopping you from making a living out of affiliate marketing.

5. It can be done parallel to other online businesses.

Many people are doing online business, and affiliate marketing can be integrated into another income stream. Since all you require is an affiliate link that can be placed anywhere on a website, it doesn't have to interfere with anything. Email marketing is automated; therefore one can earn without checking in.

Disadvantages of Affiliate Marketing

1. It takes some time before someone gets to earn money. For those who think that affiliate marketing is getting rich quick scheme, they shall be disappointed as some people have stayed for a year before making any money. It requires patience and perseverance.

2. As with any money-making venture, some people hijack your affiliate, and you don't get your commission when they use your link. To be safe, you can try using URL masking to protect your affiliate links from cybercriminals.

3. Choosing a bad affiliate company can tarnish your reputation and will lead to mistrust among your loyal followers. Ensure you work with brands that have the same value as you.

4. You cannot analyze the numbers apart from the traffic that is going to the product site, sales, and returns. You won't know anything else about the customer. Therefore, marketing will always be by chance. You are not a part of the business module unless you are the product creator.

5. Unless you are in a reputable affiliate network, you may not be paid for your work, and there is no way to track down the company.

6. It is a competitive space to be in especially if a company is offering a high commission. The challenge is how you can market the product while standing out from the rest.

Mistakes to Avoid as A New Affiliate Marketer

Don't be that person that is only looking to make a quick buck from people. People can always tell if all you are doing is pushing a product instead of being yourself. Don't think of yourself as a seller of the product but as an influence of people towards a product. All you have to do is offer a suggestion with all the relevant facts and let the people decide. If you can, test out the products first before recommending them to your loyal subscribers to avoid unforeseen problems. Don't embellish or oversell something if you are not sure how it works. It is a sure way to lose credibility.

Pick one affiliate program and perfect that instead of joining multiple programs. As a beginner, you are still wet behind the ears, and you need to learn and make mistakes before you can fill your plate with more work. Learn from other people doing the same thing on the internet and be good at one thing first. You will find out that you can make more money that way than dipping your toe in everything.

If you are promoting multiple products, track each one of them so that you can drop whatever is not earning you anything. There is no need to keep pushing something that is not converting well in sales. With a good affiliate network like Amazon, they offer unique tracking IDs that can help you manage all your links.

Avoid changing niches at all costs. When you have good subscribership, they expect something from you, and that is why they are following you. Even if you suspect something is better than what you are currently doing, make a different site for it instead of confusing your followers. See one thing through before moving on to something else.

Chapter 3
Passive Income Investments

Compound interest is the eighth wonder of the world. He who understands it earns it ... he who doesn't ... pays it. Compound interest is the most powerful force in the universe. Compound interest is the greatest mathematical discovery of all time. - Albert Einstein

What Are Passive Income Investments?

Passive income investing is where you put up your money in capital investments such as mutual funds, treasury bonds, and bills, fixed accounts and even stocks. You earn an income from either earning a percentage of the company you are investing in or you earn dividends or interest from the money you choose to invest. Here, you are just financing the investing and not directly managing it, making it passive. You will be earning residual income that is calculated by compounding what you choose to invest. As a beginner, you will only put in your money once into a passive income investment and from there on out, you will have regular deposits from your investments.

People who are working tend to ignore the fact that they won't be working forever. They need to start planning for retirement by looking into their income, their daily expenses and how much money they can save to maintain the same lifestyle when they retire. Young people are notorious for living large and forgetting that this is the best time to start saving as they have no real obligations. Investing doesn't have an age limit. Some parents open up education funds for their children as soon as they born and save. This reduces the burden when the time comes to pay from school. Some teach the importance of saving by opening for them their own savings accounts. What they need to do is teach them that money can also grow on its own if placed in the right places. These children then grow while learning to invest so that they make more money.

11 Examples of Passive Income Investments

1. Crowdfunded Real Estate

For many years, we have believed that becoming a real estate mogul requires a lot of capital to get into. An easier way to get into real estate is by investing in crowdfunded ventures. There are multiple companies like Fundraiser that allow you to deposit as low as $500 and get a stake in at least 48 real estate projects. There are some companies like Rich Uncles that you can register for free that offer even more affordable options. Rich Uncles, for example, has an offer called Student Housing REIT (Real Estate Investment Trust) that one can invest as little as $5. Many companies are trying to bring real estate investments more mainstream and are targeting low-income earners.

2. Certificate of Deposit (CDs) Ladders

CDs are a great way for beginners to start because there are no minimums in what one can start with compared to many other capital investments. The fact that they are also available in local banks is perfect as you can open a CD account easily. It is low risk because an FDIC insures individual CDs for up to $250,000 and joint accounts for up to $500,000. It's relatively easy to withdraw your money from a CD and is a great way to earn an income with minimum effort. The longer the CD like five years or more, the higher the interest the bank offers on it. You can buy CDs in online banks such as CIT bank.

3. Dividend Income

When you invest in a company by buying the shares or stocks in that company, then you earn a dividend based on the number of shares you have. If you want to learn a lot about investment, you might want to follow the billionaire investor Warren Buffet as he has a lot of wisdom to share in the subject. Dividends can be paid quarterly or annually depending on the company in question. Before investing in a company, look at their history and expert predictions on their future so that you don't end up investing in a company that won't be around for a long time. To make more money, consider investing for the long haul. To invest in stocks, open an investment account with a licensed stockbroker so that your investment is safe. You will have to pay a small fee to buy stocks, but that is all. Keep looking into good companies to invest in as you build your portfolio.

4. Bonds (Fixed Income)

Bonds are great as their interest rates were going up for the past few years. Even if the interest rates remain steady or go up, bonds are a good way to earn passive income, especially if you hold them until they mature. They are good for long term investors who will not withdraw the money before the maturity period is up. There are different bonds to choose from such as an individual corporate bond, the 7-10-year IEF, municipal bonds or the Pimco Total Return Fund which is a fixed income fund.

5. Peer to Peer Lending (P2P)

You can become a shylock of some sort, i.e., lending to people who need credit but cannot get it from traditional loan institutions. Some companies that allow you to invest in their peer to peer lending business with low costing bonds (as low as $10) and paying out returns ranging from 3-8%. They have no restriction on when you can have your money back. You can just walk in and withdraw any amount you want. It is a risky business as some borrowers will not pay back the money they borrow. You will also need to invest a lot more money to get high-interest rates.

6. Private Equity Investments

Some people had struck big because they believed in the vision of start-ups early on before they blew up. Look at the people that bought into Facebook, Uber, Amazon, Alibaba, Google and many others before they became the giants they are today. It is tough today to know which company would blow up. Therefore, you can choose to go the way other private investment firms are going. This is however not for everyone as it is limited to approved investors. They mostly invest in hedge funds, real estate, and other private companies. It is good for long term investors, and you will find more passive income. The risk depends on the company you are investing in, i.e., if it is in a competitive field like finance. Real estate and fixed income funds can give up to 8-15% interest on investments.

7. High-Yield Online Accounts

If you are looking into a low-risk investment, open an FDIC insured high yield online account with banks like CIT Bank that offer up to 2.45% interest rates. You will not earn a lot of money at once, but in the long term, you will have earned much more than if you put your money in a normal savings account. Online banks offer good interest rates as they do not have a lot of overhead to keep operating. They can pay 19 times the interest most traditional banks to pay.

8. Money Market Funds

A money market fund is perfect for beginners who have no idea what investing is all about. All you have to do is look for a reputable money market fund that offers good returns, and they will do all the thinking for you. They are located in banks and other investment agencies. There are some types of mutual funds called index funds that mirror the market index they are tied to. These funds track a certain index thus doesn't need a lot of management because the underlying index rarely changes. The fees for this fund is low, and the lower turnover means that the tax will less too. Lower taxes mean higher returns for the investor.

9. Owning a Real Estate Property

It would be unwise to assume that all beginners have no money to make big investments such as real estate. Owning a real estate property and earning a rental income has been done for a long time and it works. If you have a spare room, you can rent it out to a trustworthy tenant. You can also own a rental property and earn a steady income while it keeps increasing in value. Remember that your rental income would be subject to taxes, mortgages, insurance, and operational costs. The rental income in cities can be low because the expenses are high despite the rental income being high as well. This means that the risk of owning rental property in an expensive city is higher than owning one in a cheaper area. The same applies in areas with insecurity even with property insurance. You can also buy houses fix them up for sale at a higher cost. This is a great way to earn more money even though you may need to be involved even if you hire someone to help you out. The return is amazing, and the risk is moderate depending on the location of the property.

10. Annuities

They are offered by insurance companies where you have to pay a certain amount every month, and in return, they pay you monthly dividends. It is always better to talk to a professional finance officer before investing in annuities because not all of them are as good as they sound. Look at the terms before buying because some charge a lot and may not be a good investment. It is okay if you are looking for a zero-risk investment and want to be earning an income for a long time.

11. Pay Off Your Debts

You can be earning a steady passive income, but if all of it is going towards repaying debts and mortgages then, you are not benefitting at all. For mortgages, look for companies that are offering better rates than your current financiers. There are services online that help you compare rates for different mortgage lenders such as LendingTree. If you are repaying a credit card debt or loan at an interest rate of 12%, the good thing about repaying it is that you get a 12% straight return. You may not necessarily have a lot of money at hand. Therefore, it is better to look at two possible approaches. One is the one we have talked about earlier on refinancing the debt to one that offers a lower interest rate. The second way is to consolidate two debts and pay the two together at a lower interest rate. The third way is to register for a balance transfer card that allows you to pay off the debt within a specified period at no extra cost.

Advantages

1. You can choose what works for you. Depending on your income bracket, there are many investment options out there for you.

2. Building your investment portfolio can be an asset in the long run as you can leverage it when you need to. You may even retire if your passive investments make enough money for you to live comfortably on.

3. It is perfect for people who don't understand anything about the markets. Most of the investment is often made by trained professionals making it perfect for earning without managing anything. It is safe to say that even though someone else handles your investments, you should keep track to see if you are gaining or losing.

4. Long term investors benefit more from investments because they earn more dividends. Also, some funds also give better interest rates for investors.

Disadvantages

1. It is not exactly the quickest way to make money. It requires patience and a sound strategy to earn a good income even in the long term.

2. Even though some investments promise high yield, if you look at the return you get in the long haul, you will realize that it was not worth your time in the first place. This means that before investing, a professional would help you better understand the projections before you commit your money in a venture that won't give you high returns eventually.

3. For a beginner with little money and no expertise, high returns may be elusive. Those who earn better incomes are those who are willing to risk a lot and work to get better deals. Research and

participation may be the only way to earn a better income.

4. Investing can be quite a hard topic for people who are not into finance and economics. There are hard terms to understand, and the mathematics can be even more confusing but what separates someone who makes a wise investment from one who goes with the wind is some basic form of investing knowledge.

5. Some people ignore retirement accounts as a form of investing and yet they are low risk and are taxed a lot less than other investment accounts. Good retirement funds include 401(k)s and Roth IRAs.

6. Most people just put away money in investment accounts and forget to use some of it. It is okay to use some of the money you earn on yourself. Don't wait until you are too old to enjoy the money that you have worked so hard because other people will.

Chapter 4
Leverage Social Media

"He who makes $25,000 annually through passive income is more enviable than he who earns $100,000 annually through a salary."

— *Mokokoma Mokhonoana*

Everyone and their grandmother are on social media nowadays. The opportunities created by social media as a new kind of jobs and businesses have emerged thanks to social media. People across the globe can communicate with ease nowadays thanks to many social networks out there. There is also something for everyone depending on what you are into. If you want to connect with family and friends, Facebook might be for you. If you want to know what is happening now or trending, then you might be a Twitter person. Those that like to share their day to day lives through short videos can consider Snapchat. Instagram is for the people that value photography and beautiful aesthetics while Pinterest is what you may want your life to look like. It offers ideas on décor, fashion while still being informative. For those that want to learn how to do anything and connect with people with similar interest, consider YouTube. If you are into messaging and sharing funny memes, WhatsApp may be more up your alley. These are just a few of the popular social media sites out there, and more are coming up every day.

With Facebook having 2 billion, Instagram with 800 million and Twitter with 330 million active users every month, it is no wonder many companies have stopped ignoring social media as a place to market their products. As of 2017, many big companies and SMEs had added more money to their social media marketing budgets. Since then, more and more companies have recognized the power of influencers is selling their product on social media.

How to Find your Niche on Social Media

It's sad to say that there is nothing new that you can come up with to attract an audience on social media today. Everyone does the same things, but they add their personality to it. All you need to do is look for something that you are good at and are willing to pursue it to the end and do it better than any other person in that niche. If you want to be a makeup artist, learn the craft and do something different that people have not seen before.

Creativity on social media is what separates those who make it from those who don't. It is good to stick to one niche at a time on social media so that you can grow and become an authority on that niche. Be the person people search for when they are looking for new techniques to apply to make up for example. Be the one to put people on new products in the market. This way people trust your opinion and brands recognize your influence over your community. You can use this influence to get paid to introduce new products to your audience.

There is also such a thing as being too niche. People get bored quickly if they can predict the next content. Be unpredictable but don't stray too far from your niche. It's also good to look at what other people in your niche are doing so that you can get a clear view of where your niche is at. Look at what is popular and incorporate it but also consider what is missing and add that to your content. Research and see if your niche is scalable and leverage your audience to make yourself some money.

After picking a niche you know, you can be good at, ensure you pick the right social media platform for you to start working on. I know it is tempting to be visible on all social media platforms but it rare for someone to do a good job if they are giving less than 100% on each platform. At most, pick two of your favorite and work on those. Once you have a following, your followers you follow you wherever you are. Pick a platform that suits your niche. If it requires visuals consider YouTube, If it requires an online store, Facebook and Instagram may do the job.

Case Study: How to Make Money on Instagram

Let's look at one social media platform and see how you can make money from it. Instagram was initially as a platform to share photos with family and friends, but it has transformed to be more professional. Large and small businesses alike are using the platform to attract more customers. Some people have been able to leverage the business side of Instagram and their followers to make a good living off it.

- Leveraging higher numbers

An account with more following and a good engagement can reach out to smaller accounts in the same niche and offer to help them out at a fee. It may be mentions or a collaborative post depending on the terms agreed, but the smaller channel will get quite some followers from the larger account. This will only work if the two accounts have similar content and niches because followers will only follow what they are into. There are also niche engagement groups on Telegram and Instagram's Direct Message that charge a one-time fee to join where small accounts can interact with more influential accounts. They offer engagement boosts where people in the group can collaborate, make money and connect with each other.

- Sponsored Content

We have all seen that #ad on some of our favorite personality's posts. That means that they are collaborating with a product to introduce a product to their audience. It can either be a video, a mention or a series of posts depending on what the person and the brand agreed upon. The person called a social media influencer gets paid a certain amount to put up that post on their account. They may be seen in an event hosted by the brand, they may take photos with the photo they are advertising, or they may do a full review of the product. Larger accounts can charge a company by the hour the post stays up on their page while some may charge per post. The influencer charges based on the social reach, potential leads and eventual customers that buy from the brand from their following. With Instagram, companies can either pay for advertisement on your feed or on Instagram stories. It is important to sign contracts with the brand you are working with so that you ensure you get paid for your work. A contract is also important because it clearly states what is required of both parties.

- Flipping Instagram Accounts

It is a familiar process where an influencer can buy a small account, grow its followership and sell it at a higher price. They don't have to do a lot because they can boost engagement from their account. It is still a slow process, but it gives better returns.

- Selling your Products

If you have the numbers and already know how to market on Instagram, the next step is selling your products to your audience. You already know what they like and have enough feedback to create a product that solves a problem. You can also open an online store and start selling to your followers which is a way many people are making money on Instagram. Since Instagram is a visual platform, many creatives have used it to market their art. Photographers and videographers are some of the people that have benefitted the most from showcasing their work on the platform. People have gotten high paying contracts to work with some of the biggest brands by tagging them on work; the creator thinks the brand may like. Apps like Stylinity allow your followers to purchase content from their favorite influencers. With every purchase that is made, you can earn a commission from soothing that is already free on your page.

- Managing Other People's Instagram Accounts

If you have been on Instagram for a while and understand its algorithm, it can be easy for you to become a social media manager. You just have to take the content which the owner of the account sends you and post it at the best time with appropriate content. Depending on your arrangement, you may also handle replying to comments and direct messages. Social media management is a freelance skill that is in high demand today especially for big companies or personalities that don't have the time to deal with social media themselves. Some companies that offer services hire social media managers to answer peoples queries online and offer solutions. You can also be a consultant and offer advice to passional brands on the best strategies to grow and connect with their audience.

- Being a Brand Ambassador

This is quite similar to sponsored posts except you are the face of the brand. You will be required to attend launches and regularly speak about the brand to your audience. You will also need to use the brand's product exclusively depending on what is agreed upon by both parties. In exchange, the influencer gets paid regularly by the company. Look for unique brands an approach them for a long-term partnership. The best way to land a brand ambassador job is if you grow your personal brand and have a target following that a brand may want to associate with.

- Affiliate Marketing

You can promote products on your page by linking their links wither in the bio space or on Instagram Stories. People are more likely to buy if you give an honest view of the products and it solves a need they have. They will also buy if it is in your page's niche.

How to Grow Your Social Media Following

1. Consistency

No matter how good your content may be, your followers still require you to come up with new content regularly. If it is video content, make a routine such that your followers can know when to expect new content. Even social media algorithms favor people that are more consistent and suggest the accounts to more people.

2. Authenticity

The pressure to get more followers makes people do crazy things for likes and follows. People tend to copy people that are doing well in the hopes that they will get more followers. The truth is that people are not stupid, and they can separate who is real and who is fake. You may gain some followers that way but keeping them is a real challenge especially if you don't know what you are doing. Don't fake it till you make it on social media because it will backfire on you.

3. Link All your Social Media Accounts

People prefer different social media platforms, and you can still leverage that with the content you post. By linking all your social media accounts, you don't need to keep posting the same stuff all over your platforms because there are apps available for that now. Some people will also start following you in one platform because they saw your content on another platform.

4. Host Campaigns, Giveaways, and Competitions

The point of social media is to have fun, and people enjoy accounts that have interesting things going on. If you are creative, you can come up with fun competitions that your followers can participate in where the winner goes home with something nice. This is also a way you can promote products to your followers because you get to introduce the product through giveaways for the winners to try them out. Your followers will share the competitions and campaigns with their friends and that you will gain new followers.

5. Interact and Collaborate

The good things about social media are that it doesn't discriminate who the audience is. You can talk to people in your niche and learn from them how they grew their following. You can also collaborate on different projects on each other's pages and earn followers from one another. Remember that no one owes you anything and they are not obligated to working with you. You can start by being friendly and supporting their content online such as liking their pictures, sharing it and engaging with them in the comments and direct messages. A good and profitable business relationship is the one that is cultivated through legitimate friendship.

6. Hashtags

Since their inception, hashtags have been able to connect people with the same interests and likes. There is a community for just about anything online and the best way to find it is through social media hashtags. You can add popular hashtags in your content or simply the ones that are relevant to your niche and the people who like your content will stay. If you are promoting something, you can create your hashtag and encourage people to jump on it. You never know, it may go viral.

7. Use Geotags

The same way hashtags connect people with similar likes and interests, so do geotag with people in the same location. All social media sites have a way to add where you are posting on, and other people can see it too.

8. Use Insights and Analytics on your Site

Analytics and insights are very important for someone who considers social media in a business sense. It allows the account holder to look at what the audience likes and what they do not. It also tells him or her who is interested in their content, where they are from and even the best time to post. Some even apps can even tell which other social media sites new followers are coming from. With all this information, it easier to plan your content to suit the demand, making your page more appealing to people and brands.

9. Make More Video Content

All social media platforms are embracing the power of video content. YouTube gained a lot of popularity as people could relate to content because they could see the person they like and their personality. Other social media platforms have added similar functionalities where the user can add short videos. It is also believed that video is the future of advertising as more and more people prefer are moving away from print media and written work.

10. Paying for Advertisement

Social media sites earn the majority of their income through paid advertisements on their platforms. They also offer advertising or their users to reach people with similar interests. Paid advertising on social media is relatively cheap considering the amount of reach you get. And that doesn't even account for the sharing that would ensue if people like your product or content.

11. Quality Content

They say content is king and I agree. There is no shortcut when it comes to providing quality to your followers. If you want the ones you have to stick around, it is better to give them the best as opposed to doing everything else to add more followers. People will always join if they see something they like. Even if you are selling things, do it subtly or incorporate it in what you already do instead of making your page look like a billboard. People always notice shifts in your content especially those that have been with you for a while.

A disclaimer here is that there are plenty of cons and scam artists that will approach you and your growing account and claim that they can sell you like, followers and other things but it is not worth it. These are bots that have no real value especially if you think of your account as a business. You need to account to grow organically so that the engagement and feedback are real so that you can leverage that in the future. Growing your social media pages will take time, but when you have a genuine following, you can make bank.

Ralf Percy

Chapter 5
Making Money from Websites

To obtain financial freedom, one must be either a business owner, an investor or both, generating passive income, particularly on a monthly basis.

Robert Kiyosaki

The internet is full of websites on different niches and topics. There are two ways to make money from domains: One, buy a new domain, and then sell it and two, buy an expired domain, then sell it. Both of these methods can be called domain flipping. There is also another way where one purchases the domains, works on the website and grows it and later sell it at a higher price with content and traffic. That is called website flipping. Domain flipping is relatively cheaper because all you need to do is buy a good domain name that can be sold later at a higher price. With website flipping, one spends a lot of time and resources raising it from the ground up, and the returns are much higher than domain flipping. There are those people that will buy websites to flip and that can be risky because it may not be as lucrative especially for a beginner. Domain flipping is easier because one has to identify good expired domain names, buy them and keep them till a good deal comes along. Domain flipping is faster because there isn't a lot of details to it; all one needs is an interest in the domain name, and the deal can be finalized. The same can't be said about websites because there is a lot to consider before someone makes the purchase. As a beginner, you can start with domain flipping and learn the ropes on what is lucrative, and what isn't. You can also learn what to do if you eventually decide to start flipping websites. You will learn where you can buy and sell websites because of experience and know-how.

What Makes a Domain Name Lucrative?

For a beginner, the main question will be, how can I tell if a domain name is profitable or not? There are certain elements that you need to look at when selecting lucrative domain names:

- How long is the domain name? As I said before, the internet has a lot of websites, and most of the short domain names are taken already. Therefore, if you get a domain name with 3-4 letters, it is valuable because it's unlikely you will find one that isn't already taken. These domain names are valuable because they can be an exact match to the name of a brand or a company.

- How old is it? The older the domain name (one registered over ten years ago), the more likely to have a lot of backlinks. Backlinks are a sign a website has authority. Therefore, both age and authority can determine the price of a domain name.

- Can it make a brand? When looking at short domain name with random letter combinations, look at it critically to see if it can be used in branding. Some are more straightforward than others.

- Is the domain extension on the domain name valuable? The domain name can have 3-4 letters and may seem perfect but look at its extension. Look for domains with popular extensions such as .com, .gov, .edu, .net, .org etc. There are uncommon extensions that can still work so don't rule anything out.

- Are the words in the domain name searched on search engines?

You should consider taking domains that have a high search volume on popular search engines such as google.com. That means that the domain will be on demand.

- Does the domain name contain a popular term? Many businesses and brands are coming up every day so you should choose a name that could be of interest. You need to discern because a business may not exist now, but the domain name could still be valuable. Even if the domain name is highly searched, it should also have low competition among the searches to ensure uniqueness. Look at all these aspects on a keyword planner to make the right choice.

- Is the domain name the name of a person? You never know if a person may be interested in a domain name of their name to create a personal brand.

There are two ways to determine if a domain name is valuable enough to buy: Buying domains based on popular topics or based on how exclusive they are. Topic-based domains are lucrative because they can contain the name of a popular niche, business or brand that would be easy to flip. Exclusive domain names are lucrative because they are one of a kind and can never be registered again. Common words and 3-4 letter combos are exclusive as they were registered at the inception of the internet.

How to Start Domain Flipping

1. Find expired domain names

The internet has many domain name marketplaces where one can search and buy expired domain names. Domain names expire when its owner forgets to renew it with the domain registrar. The domain registrar is the service provider that registered the domain name in the first place. When the domain name is not registered, the domain registrar offers a grace period, usually 30 days where the owner can still pay and retain his or her domain. If no payment is made in the time stipulated, the domain registrar lists the domain in a public auction. The buyer has to check for the following before buying the expired domain:

- Domain Authority (DA)

This is an SEO metric that assigns a value between 1-100 that shows how high on a search engine the website would rank. Number 1 is the highest score while 100 is the lowest. Moz.com came up with this metric system by looking at the count of backlinks to the site, its social signal, the quality of the content in the website the Moz Rank and Trust and how easily the search engine crawler can maneuver in the website. DA looks at the whole website.

- Page Authority (PA)

Here, the page is the focus of the evaluation.

- The Quality and Count of Backlinks/ SEO Profile

The older a domain, the more the backlinks it will have. Even if it has a lot of backlinks, they should also be of good quality, i.e. they should be legitimate. A poor-quality backlink is full of spam from suspicious referring websites and too many backlinks coming from suspicious niche websites from using services from Private Blog Networks (PBN) and not organic backlinking from good quality websites. There are research tools that can help you do extensive backlink research such as Ahrefs or moz.com.

- The History of the Domain of the Expired Website.

Investigate if there were other owners of the domain name before the previous owner. Some 3-4 letter domain names may have been used for other things before landing on the auction. Therefore, it's better to research before buying a domain name with baggage. Use archive.com to confirm its safe to buy.

- Bans on Google

Check if AdSense or Google banned your domain name before buying, otherwise you might not get a buyer for it. Use isbanned.com to find out if it was banned from google the search engine and bannedcheck.com to rule out a ban from Google AdSense.

2. Buy Expired Domain Names

There are many websites online that offer domain auctions. Remember that some of them may require you to pay a monthly fee to participate. Some websites include DomCop, ExpiredDomains, Domain Hunter Gatherer, Domainhole.com, Godaddy.com, Dropcatch.com, JustDropped.com among others. You can also save some money when buying expired domain names by using promo codes using Groupon.com.

3. Sell your Domain Name

There are a few marketplaces that you can sell your domain names, for example, Bido.com, Flippa, Namepros.com or Sedo.com. If you have built a domain flipping niche website, you might want to sell to your email list subscribers.

4. Set a Price for your Domain Name

As we had discussed earlier, the price of each domain name depends on many other factors, not just the buying price. If it in demand, if it is exclusive or if it brandable; all these are factors that can be used to set the price of your domain. You can also listen to the price the potential buyer is offering and then negotiate. With time, you will be able to tell the price point each domain lies depending on the market. The price of domains differs from that of websites. The value of a website is in the traffic it receives in a specified period, its content, current and potential revenue and the SEO profile of the website. When in doubt consult an agency that can run an analysis and give you the estimate of the website.

5. Use Expired Domain Names for your Own Website

Some people look for expired domain names for more than just flipping. You can buy an authoritative domain name and start your blog with it. Some people buy expired domain names and use them for their backlink potential. You can do this using 301 redirect which links the domain name to your website when someone clicks on it. Some of the old domain names are better than registering new domain names. Using parking service providers, you can earn from advertisements on the domain name website especially if it receives traffic from errors and referral traffic sources. Using expired domain name websites, you can build your own PBN by directing them to your website. However, you have to be careful not to appear like your website is being spammed which can do more harm than good in the long run.

How to Start Website Flipping

1. Pick a Niche that you will Focus on.

The niche of your website should be based on your passion and knowledge. You can also pick a popular niche that people are searching for online. The niche should be evergreen such that people will always be looking for it online for a long time to come. This ensures you keep earning a passive income for a long time.

2. Choose Main Keywords

Use a free or premium Keyword Planner to determine the keywords that you will need to use in your website for SEO purposes. It should also have low competition (less than 100000) so that it can stand out from other websites in the same niche.

3. Add Supporting Keywords

From the main keyword, you will need another 15 keywords or more that are more or less related to the main keyword so that you can write content based on them. The more the articles, the better you will earn in the future.

4. Buy a Domain Name with your Keywords

If your domain name matches the keywords you have selected, then your website with rank high on google searches. You can either do this first and work backward or hope that you get something in the niche you have chosen. Either way, a good domain name coupled with a good extension such as .com or .net will rank faster on search engines.

5. Write Content for the Website

Pick a template that allows for AdSense and starts working on content. You should have 50-70 500-word articles published on your website. Use your keywords at least three times; in the title, in the first and last paragraphs and in the body. Use one keyword per article.

6. Submit your Website Online

Don't just post your website and hope that the search engine crawlers find your work. This may take a long time because your website is still new. Submit your work straight to the submission websites of all the popular search engines you know.

7. Market your Website Online

Now you need traffic leading to your website. You need to find people that are looking for your niche through social media websites and other websites. You can also try guest posting on authority sites to get backlinks to your website. Try as much as you can to earn quality backlinks to help your website.

8. Earn Through AdSense.

Apply for AdSense and ensure that your website is ranking on the top page of all search engines.

9. Put it on Sale

There are websites that you can list your website on sale such as Sitepoint.com. If your website is ranking on the top page and has good quality content, then you are on your way to making the sale. Add the passive income that it is already generating then you will have hit the jackpot.

Chapter 6
eBook Publishing

You become financially free when your passive income exceeds your expenses.

T. Harv Eker

Writing a Book

Writing an eBook is not easy, and it definitely requires some commitment. You require a month onward to write a book from start to finish. First and foremost, you have to consider what you are passionate about. As I said, writing isn't as easy as many people make it seem. It is even harder to write about a topic you know nothing about. Consider your experience, skills, knowledge on a certain topic and expertise.

You will need to allocate time to do your research on what you want to write and see if there is a market for it. Look for keywords that are popular in the genre you want to write about and create a concept you think people would be interested in. For nonfiction, consider what is popular, but for nonfiction, there is a wide range of categories to choose from on self-publishing sites. The secret here is to know when to put it up.

The next stage is to look for an interesting and catchy title that suits your theme and is easy to remember. This is more important for fiction because it's what people will remember your book as. Nonfiction is more lenient because you only have to include the popular keyword on the title. Use your title to tell the audience what they will be getting from your book. Include the time frame to make it more enticing, like How to Earn $1000 a Week Selling eBooks in 2019.

If you have all that, then it's time to plan what you are going to write. I insist, content is king and should be what matters most in your book. Whether you decide on a long or short book, you should add value to the reader with your content. At this point, it is good to consider taking an online writing course if you are not a confident writer. Have an outline of what your book is about that you can follow until you complete the book. Remember that you can add and subtract what you want from the outline as you write the book.

After writing the book, you might want to read through and fix some plot holes, especially in fiction. You can get some beta readers that can help you with your story. Once you are confident that your story is okay, move on to grammar. Use any grammar checking tools and fix common mistakes. You can go a step further and hire a professional editor to help you out. Now it's time to start with the publishing process.

Self-Publishing an eBook

Many people are fooled to believe that self-publishing their own way is an excuse not to work hard. After all, it's just posting it on one of the many self-publishing sites and that it. Wrong! You will need to brace yourself for the long and gruesome work ahead of you so that you are well prepared. However, this is not to discourage anyone not to pursue this option to publish their book. Self-publishing is the only option for man people because there are very few traditional publishers that are taking chances on new, inexperienced writes nowadays. Since the option of doing it yourself is available, why not try it. If you are determined and willing to put in the work, then, this is the process for you.

1. Format your Document into an eBook Readable Format

When you are writing, you will probably use a word processing document and format using the same. This is okay if it were to be read using the same word document, but since it isn't, the formatting will have to be different. You want your book to be readable by any eBook reader available in the market because readers won't have the one you use. There is no need to use headers, footers or page numbers in an eBook. This is because the reader is not keen on page numbers and the eBook reader will add its own headers and footers. Your headings should have heading styles so that the reader will acknowledge topics and subtopics. Your paragraphs should be formatted using the first-line indentation to make the reader flow seamlessly from one paragraph to another. Remember to separate one chapter from another using page breaks. The same can be done for sections. Your images should be of the.jpg format, and they should not be wrapped. You can add them to the center as inline images. There should be an individual page that shows your title and subtitle and another separate on showing copyright instructions. The ISBN number can either be displayed on the title page or the copyright page. The next page should show your book's Table of Contents to inform the reader what to expect in the book. The use of heading styles makes generating a table of content very easy. Your cover page/ image should be the first page of the book.

2. Make an eBook Cover that Suits your Book and is Attractive to the Reader

I'm sure you have heard the proverb don't judge a book by its cover. Well, they were wrong in this instance because many people will judge your work by the cover you present them. The more attractive the cover is, the more likely people will purchase your book. In this step, ensure that you take some time and come up with something everyone will love.

There are two ways to get an eBook cover for your book. The first one is probably the easiest, i.e., hire a professional to do it. There are countless freelance sites where you can get an expert to do the work for you at an affordable rate. They even come up with multiple samples for you to choose the one you like the most. The second ay may be time-consuming but if you are creative can be enjoyable.

To create your eBook cover, remember that you will need an image of 1659px by 2500px, the size of the width and length respectively. Some sites may ask for a smaller image; therefore it's up to you to do your research. Don't put a border around the image. Use the standard RBG (red, blue and green) color index for your image. Add the title of the book and the author's name in a font everyone can read. Don't use too much calligraphy so that everyone can understand. Avoid pixelating the image and stay away from profane images.

3. Convert your Document to eBook Readable Format

There are many conversion software's out there that allows you to convert your book to acceptable formats such as .epub, .mobi, and .pdf. The .pdf format is quite easy because most word processors allow you to export your document in this format. Even if they don't, there are plenty of software on the internet that can even do that for free. The .mobi format is available to the Calibre word processor. You are not required to do the conversion yourself as the software will do it for you although in some instances the results may not be to your liking. This format is only acceptable to Amazon and Amazon will convert it into .epub format. The .epub format is a little bit more complex than the other two. You can follow instructions online on how to convert to from .doc to .epub formats, or you can take the easier route and search online for conversion software.

4. Check your Cover Before Uploading it Anywhere

Once you have converted your book into the .epub format, you will still need to see if it looks good. You can download the formatted image and use an eBook reader to open the document and see it is up to standard. The major places that should be of interest are the cover image, the table of contents, the images in the book, bullets, and numbering and all pages of the book should be in the formatted book.

5. Do Some Final Touch-ups if your Book Needs it.

In case you found some mistakes, there is software such as Sigil that you can use to make your changes. If the book is acceptable in your standards, you can publish on one of the following sites.

- Amazon Kindle,
- Apple on iTunes
- Barnes & Noble,
- Ingram
- Scribd
- Google Play
- or Baker and Taylor

A Step by Step Guide to Marketing an eBook

Months before the launch

There is no specific time to start promoting your book. The earlier you start, the better, even if you just had the idea. This is because you can involve your readers in the process so that they look forward to the day you launch the book to them. You can also get some feedback along the way to improve your writing process. The best way to do this is through a social media platform. Find the sites your readers could be on and when are they online. You can also check to see what they like to read. You should definitely have a Facebook account and one on Goodreads. Start on branding as soon as possible to create a community of people that will back you up. Get people to sign up to your email list. This should happen approximately 2-3 months. If you have something to show your audience, do so at this time like excerpts, book cover or launch date. Get them excited about the book.

A month to the launch

Have influential people talk about your upcoming book or launch date. If you are done, this is the time to start sending free samples to some people. Give them a week to read and follow up with questions. You can ask some bloggers to review your book and don't forget to thank them. Ask them to rate your book on Amazon so that your book ranks at the top when it is launched. On sites like Goodreads, Amazon, Publish Drive's platform makes your book available for preorder and set a launch date. Choose a less competitive genre or two for your book. Use YouTube to show a book trailer which is a trend with today's writers.

One week to the launch

You are almost at the end, and this is where the marketing should get more intense. Start using your email list by sending them reminders of your launch. Get vigilant on social media and get people to start talking about your book. Depending on your resources you can issue a press release or just pay people to generate a buzz around your launch. At this point, it is better to start assembling a launch team to help you on the day of the launch.

The Launch

The best way to make the most sales from your book is by adhering to look for the best time to put up your book. Consider the following timetable for different genres.

- January

Good genres to publish are; motivation, fitness, inspiration, self-help and goal-setting.

Bad Genres to publish are; summertime books, fiction.

- February

Good genres to publish are; poetry, love, and romantic books.

Bad Genres to publish are; recipes and any other fiction that isn't focused on love and romance.

- March

Good genres to publish are; baseball and most sports genres, women-focused books.

Bad Genres to publish are; Travel and self-help books.

- April

Good genres to publish are; Easter and other religious books, and fiction, biographies, and memoirs, books on WWII.

Bad Genres to publish are; Winter and holiday books, fiction on love and romance.

- May

Good genres to publish are; Parenting books, Fiction, history, and summer-based books.

Bad Genres to publish are; Fiction on love and romance, self-help books.

- June

Good genres to publish are; Books on parenting especially fatherhood, contemporary fiction.

Bad Genres to publish are; Fitness and romance fiction.

- July and August

Good genres to publish are; Any heavy reading books, fiction.

Bad Genres to publish are; Self-help books, holiday books.

- September

Good genres to publish are; Books on memoirs, politics, history, college, and school (Educational reads.)

Bad Genres to publish are; Fiction, especially love and romance.

- October

Good genres to publish are; Dark non-fiction especially mysteries, thrillers, and horror.

Bad Genres to publish are; Fiction, especially love, romance and fairy tale relationships.

- November

Good genres to publish are; Children's books, holiday books, recipe, and cookbooks, religious books.

Bad Genres to publish are; Fiction especially love and romance, self-help books.

- December

Good genres to publish are; Don't put up anything.

Bad Genres to publish are; Most books.

Remember to have fun, talk to people and connect. Answer questions people may have on your book at all times during that day.

One week after the launch

It's time to show gratitude to people who worked with you before the launch, during the launch and after. If by now you have started getting reviews, remember to thank them too. Now that you have a book look for ways to market it online. Search the internet for programs that will help you market to more people.

One month after the launch

Your sales are not going to be on an upward movement, and it is time to start offering sales and discounted deals to keep people interested. The book will enjoy a spike in sales, but after that, it's better just to let your network do the marketing for you. This will only happen if your book is good.

Chapter 7
Renting Your Belongings

Make money, don't let the money make you. Change the game; don't let the game change you.

Macklemore

Most of us have too many things that we don't use just lying around. There is a market out there for renting out things we no longer use but are still in working condition. This may be confusing because most people don't know where to start when it comes to making passive income with the items they already own. Other people are scared because there are many unsavory characters on the internet that can be dangerous. This is not to mean that you cannot get good people to pay you for using your stuff. We shall see how you can rent your stuff to make extra money.

What can you Rent Out to Make Some Money?

1. Rent Out Your Wedding Gown

It is absurd how much a wedding dress costs especially because you can only wear it once. That is the reason some people choose to make some money by letting another bride have it for their wedding day. Some websites allow you to add a picture of the dress and once it approves, you will be able to earn some passive income from your dress. An example is Borrowing Magnolia that even helps you ship, clean, and maintain your wedding dress.

2. Rent your Living Space

Some people have big homes or spare rooms that can be used by tourists and visitors at a fee. Why bother looking for tenants when there are sites like Airbnb, Wimdu, HomeAway, and VBRO (vacation rental by owner) that connects a tourist to a beautiful home that they can stay in while they are visiting a place. Don't worry about damages because Airbnb covers you with close to a million dollars. They only take a small commission, and you get to keep the rest of the money. You can make arrangements with the renter on how to get the keys and deposit. Some even have the option of choosing the tenants they want in their home. There are sites like Giggster that allows you to list our home or part of your home as the potential set of a movie or television series. How cool is that!

3. Rent your Car

Some people have cars, but they don't use them often. Others have multiple vehicles and store them in the garage when they can rent it out to make money. You can register with Turo and Getaround rent out your car to people in your local area and earn a percentage of the profit. You can choose to rent it until your car reaches a certain mileage and the hour's people can rent your car. For safety reasons, you are the only one that can give the renter a code that unlocks the doors. Payments are made monthly, and they fuel your car upon return. You can also hire your car to drivers for companies such as Uber, Lyft and Hyrecar and earn more income. These apps are offer taxi services on people's cars. The car is insured and safe because the companies track them. If you have an RV in storage, there is also a market for that through RVshare that allows you to rent your mobile home at a fee. Same goes for motorbikes through Spinlister.

4. Rent your Parking Spot

If you live in a populated area or a place that experiences a lot of traffic due to events, then you might want to consider renting your parking space for some extra cash. Sites such as JustPark or ParkingSpotter can help you get a renter for your parking space. There is the option of making it a long- or short-term deal, depending on what you are comfortable with.

5. Rent your Storage Space or Garage

Some people have a garage with a lot of space that they can rent out to people with a lot of items they rarely use. If you have space and can get someone willing to rent your garage, all you have to do is get a rental agreement, and both of you sign it, and then you get to earn passive income monthly. StoreAtMyHouse and Craigslist can help you find renters for your space at a commission and free respectively. The same applies to a storage space that you may not be using that someone else needs.

6. Rent your Clothes

If you have an amazing sense of fashion and style, then this one is for you. If you have a lot of trendy outfits that you don't get to wear often, you can consider StyleLend that allows people on the website to wear your articles of clothing. They offer insurance against damage or loss. Ensure everything is in order before sending it out to the center. You can price your item from 5-10% of the items market value. They give you 80 % of the money they get.

7. Allow Campers on your Land at a Fee

Some sites that allow you to rent a home also allow campers to rent camping gear from the owner. If you also have enough land to fit a camping site imagine the amount of money you can make from both. Otherwise, Gamping connects campers to landowners who want to rent out camping space. Campers can either bring their gear or you as a renter can provide everything for them to make more money.

8. Rent your Tools

Whether you have the big tools that cost a lot of money or simple household tools like screw gun, hot glue gun, vacuum cleaner, etc., FatLAma, Zilok, T'work, PeerRenters, and Loanables are there for you to list the tools you are not using to get renters. You can rent per hour or per day that's up to you. The bigger the equipment, the more money you shall get for it. Get yourself some insurance to protect yourself against liabilities in case of injuries. Talk to the renters and ensure you get a higher deposit in case of damages. You can also rent out everyday equipment like drones, musical instruments or cameras to professionals that need them. You can use Toolsity for that.

9. Rent your Boat

People who live next to large water bodies more often than not have boats. The boats may be fishing boats or houseboats where people can spend a couple of days at the marina. Sites like GetMyBoat and BoatSetter connects people who are looking for a boat with boat owners.

10. Rent your Baby's Old Gear

Baby gear can be expensive, and since your child has already outgrown most of the fancy gear you bought, you can consider renting it out to new parents. Use BabyQuip to connect you to new parents who may need these items for their baby.

11. Rent an Event Space

If you have a yard big enough to fit a large group of people, you can consider renting it out on sites like ThisOpenSpace, Splacer or PeerSpace. You can specify the time that the events can be held in your space. Depending on the size of your space, events like birthdays, team building, wedding photoshoots, baby showers, anniversary dinners and so on can be held at your space at a fee.

12. Rent out Yourself

Yes, you heard me. Yourself. It is not a typo. People can do almost anything online and, in this case, help them find a friend in the local vicinity that they can hang out with or talk to. They can also rent friends in different parts of the world so that they have company when they are in a foreign area. RantAFriend.com allows people to find people they like to connect with as friends. You can offer your services as a friend who may include; talking, walling them around time giving private tours, giving advice, going out to parties, watching movies and dining out. You can charge by activities or number of hours, that's up to you. There is a site called BridesmaidsforHire that allows brides to hire people to be at their wedding party.

How to Earn Money Doing Stuff you Already do

There are tons of stuff we do for free that we should definitely be paid for. Some of these activities take up most of our time anyway, and it is a relief to know that we can get paid to do them. This is a very attractive offer especially for people that are in college and need the extra money. There are many companies out there that require people to help them understand the market or are just looking for feedback on their products and are willing to pay for these services. Some of the things that you already do and should be paid for include:

- Getting your Money Back for Online Shopping

For those that are into online shopping, countless cash back programs allow you to save money when you spend money on their websites. Since you already shop online, this is a good way to earn back some of that money you have already spent. One would wonder how they can give you cash back when you shop. You see, when you shop through a certain website's portal, the sellers pay a commission to said websites, They then give you a percentage of the commission because you shopped through their portal as customer appreciation. The same applies to some credit cards such as Discover it that offer cashback rewards to its customers.

- Earning Through Surfing the Internet

We are always on the internet searching for answers, looking for things and even connecting with friends. What better way to earn some extra money by using a search engine to browse the internet and getting a commission site like Qmee, Swagbucks and Inbox Dollars offer money to its customers for using their search engines.

- Earning Through Watching TV

Some apps allow you to watch an array of videos online and then reward you with points that you can redeem for many things including money. Some websites pay you to binge-watch shows, and you receive a stipend while others pay you to watch and give your honest opinion in exchange for money. Examples include Watch Netflix, Perk. Tv, National Consumer Panel, Nielsen TV ratings, Nielsen Digital Voice, Success Bux, etc.

- Save Money by Booking Hotels and Flights on Travel Websites

Even though you technically don't make money through this method, it is helping you keep the money you already have. For people that love traveling by air, you can consider using online travel sites to book your travel and accommodation to save some money.

- Earning Money Through Grocery Shopping

Many people know the money-saving art of couponing is the only way you can save money when shopping for their groceries. Additionally, some sites allow you to look for rebate products such that when you are shopping and happen to buy such a product, you can scan your receipt and get your money back. They also offer cash back rewards for their customers. An example is Ibotta.

- Earning Money for Keeping Fit

There is a mobile application focussed on wellness and fitness where you can sign up and complete certain fitness tasks for you to do. You pledge to do these tasks within a specifies period, and you get money in your account. You will, however, be fined if you fail to complete the task. This is not a problem for someone that is dedicated to fitness and working out.

Chapter 8
Making Passive Income as An Artist/Creative

If you don't find a way to make money while you sleep, you will work until you die.

Warren Buffett

The reason I chose to put artists in a separate group is that there is too much stigma facing the art industry. By art, I don't necessarily mean drawing or painting but any art form that people think one cannot make a career out of. For me, artists are those that make and sell candles, underground musicians, if you make shoes, guitars, jam, chili and so many more. They use their imaginations to make things that we need on a day to day basis. They may not have enough money to advertise, but they still want to make a living from their ideas. This chapter is meant for anyone that uses their imagination to make anything.

How to Earn a Living as An Artist or Creative

1. Stock Photography

Some people don't know that you can sell your photographs online to people. They assume that you can only get money by getting clients to pay for your skills. There are many people out there that take photos of buildings, plants, animals or landscapes that are not paid by someone to do so. They enjoy the work and would like to know how they can make more money from their photos. There are websites online that buy photographs from talented photographers. Depending on the site, the photographer can be offered a commission every time someone pays to use the photo, or the website can just give the photographer a one-time fee, and they now own the photo. If you have those beautiful pictures f your phone or DSLR camera and don't know what to do with them, you can create a portfolio and approach one of these websites, e.g., Shutterstock. Other sites include Alamy, Picfair, EyeEm, Foap, iStockphoto, Dreamstime, Free digital photo Getty Images, etc. Even if you get a commission from the website, you have no control over what the person who is licensed by the website does with it. Paying you a commission is the better deal as you will be receiving online payments as long as people use your work. How can you have your work approved by one of these websites?

- Have a theme for each photo you take and choose the best from each theme. They only need the best shot; otherwise they could reject your work because of duplication. Keep your submission to 10 photos.

- Some websites have millions of photographs, and they have different categories for each one of them. It is already hard to get in one of these websites, but it is even harder if you submit a photo in a popular category. Do something unique that they may not have seen before, and you are guaranteed to be accepted. Keep your best materials for later and start with a simple yet beautiful shot.

- Avoid submitting photos that capture brand names or trademarked items. That would cause your photo to be rejected for copyright infringement. Avoid people's faces, public places or commercial objects. You may submit them in the future if you're accepted.

- Keep your images the recommended size. Ensure that they are visible and meet the standards of the website you are submitting to.

- Edit your photo before submitting. Many software allows you to do so. You can remove vignettes, add color among other things. Never submit photos with lens flares.

2. Licensing your art to third parties

Here, you have to look for people who need your art say a photograph, music, application and sell them a license to use your product for your work. You will earn more money this way as you are the one that gets to set a price for what you think your work is worth. You will need to have a unique product and look for people that you think can buy a license for it. There are many ways to do that, i.e., through social media, email lists and sending out proposals. Don't just wait for people to stumble upon your work. You can market your work anywhere on the internet where you can reach more people faster. You get to make money licensing the product every time they renew the license while you still get to keep your product.

3. eBooks

We have talked about self-publishing and selling eBooks before in this book; therefore I shall skip through this. Although I should remind you that the book should be based on what you are doing. You can do an introduction of what you so and then be creative with your content. You can make an instruction guide or any other information you may have to share with your reader.

4. Start a Blog Related to your Art

Any business out there is required to have a website in this day and age, so should you for your art. For people to take you seriously, they need to see your portfolio or sample of what you can do before they are convinced to buy. Having a blog also allows you to apply other passive income generating avenues such as advertising, affiliate marketing, email marketing and selling your art online. You can also create a membership site that you can share with your paying audience special work and your process. You make a monthly income as opposed to making them buy something just once. You will require to do more work of creating new products to keep the members satisfied, and you will need more sophisticated software to maintain your site to manage payments and ease of use by users. Despite the workload, you will definitely earn more this way than all the other methods.

5. Make Money by Selling Social Media Shout-outs to other Smaller Artists

If you have a good following on social media, you can make money by approaching smaller talented artists and ask them if they would pay for a shout out. Some will agree, and some may not have the money to pay you so it's up to you if you can help out someone talented by using your platform for good. It is important to remember that you should only be giving shout-outs to people in your niche. You don't want to confuse your audience by introducing a different niche in your space unless it's a collaboration that is tied somehow to your niche.

6. Be a Part of an Artist Collective

It is always better to share ideas with fellow artists than going about it alone. Most people feel the need to try and make it on their own when it can be easier as a group. Artistry, for example, is one of those industries that wouldn't work properly if people failed to communicate and inspire each other. Rather than struggle as a starving artist, link up with other artists that can help you sell your product or art. With people doing similar things or even different things but in the artistic industry, you can come up with cool projects you can do together. You can start art galleries, and you can make niche groups or clubs. You and a group of your similar minded friends can look for ways you can benefit the community you live in through youth projects, teaching classes to the needy and help inspire more people to join the arts.

How to Make an Online Course and Make Money Selling It

The reason I have not included this topic of creating and selling your own online course as a way to make a passive income as an artist is that it is the main way for an artist to make money. The only thing an artist really has is the talent and what better way to leverage that talent than to package it and sell it online. Multiple platforms allow an artist to do that but before then let's look at how to create an online course.

1. Find a Subject Matter

You already identified the skill that you have and want to share with the world. Its time to look at it in-depth and see if you have enough material to fit an entire course. You will have to come with some interesting materials that people would be interested in paying you for. Create a title that includes the core skills your course will impart on your students. In your description ad two or three more core skills that you promise they will leave with after they complete your course. These are what will enable you to plan your lessons, make marketing easier and deliver your point across to your students.

2. Find Out if there is a Need

This is important because if people are not interested in the topic you want to teach, then there is no need to do it at all. This is where you can look at what people are saying online and find what else you can include in your course. You need to start learning more about our course so that you are not caught unaware when questions start coming in.

3. Make a Teaching Plan and Course Outline

You have to consider your time and when you are available for the lessons. Talk to your community online and ask them when they are free to take your course and plan around that. You then have to think of how to structure your lessons. Are they in modules or weeks? What should each module contain and how can I make it as interactive as possible? How long are each module and the course in general? Make sure you cover all the bases before you dive in.

4. Consider your Teaching Methods.

Each student is different, and you might want to cater to their different learning styles. Some learn from looking at pictures while others like working on the lessons through a quiz at the end. You can look for feedback to find the best delivery method like text, video, guides, audio, worksheets, etc. You can combine two methods to teach your course.

5. Make your Content

This s where the bulk of your work will be. You have to ensure that you deliver something useful to the people who will take your course; otherwise, you will receive a tone of bad reviews. You also have to make the workload easy for them to follow and ask questions when they don't. The videos and audio should be clear for everyone to follow what you are saying. Brand your material attractively so that people know what they are taking. After you finish the work, go through it again and make sure it is good enough for the students. Before you get cocky and think that you have created the best course ever, it's important to remember that everything you have written can be found free on the internet. Packaging your work in a convenient, easy to understand way is what makes people interested in your course. They want to know everything related to your core skills without having to consult other sources.

Here is how to sell your course online:

1. Plan How to Sell the Course

Assuming you already have a website, add the features that you will need to deliver the course to your community. If you don't, start with that. There are multiple plugins especially on WordPress that help you with the selling and delivery of an online course. If you are not skilled in making such a website, you can sell your course on other websites that already offer that service such as Skillshare or Udemy. You will, however, have to share with the website a part of your earnings depending on the sales you make. The advantages of these websites are that you don't have to worry about delivery systems as they take care of selling the course and processing payments. You will have to reduce the cost of your course because the competition can get very steep. You also don't control your work because you are not running the course. There is a better option that combines two of the different delivery styles. You get to control what the content looks like but still maintain the benefits of an online course website. Examples of such websites include Ruzuku and Teachable.

2. Upload your Course Online

Depending on the platform you choose to deliver your course, you will need to customize your course to look appealing to the students. You will have to use visible fonts, an attractive color scheme and your logo for branding purposes. People need to be able to recognize your brand.

3. Marketing

As with everything else in this book, people need to know what you are doing before they come on board. You will need to use multiple social media sites, blog, email list and many other avenues to tell people why they need to take your course. Social media has paid pay-per-click advertising options that you can pay for to reach more people in your niche. It also allows you to see who is interested in our page among other insights that can help you put together a marketing plan that suits everyone on your community. In your marketing pitches, focus more on what the students will get out of the course rather than focusing on selling the course itself. You can tell them what to expect if they take the course. If you have other courses, offer them testimonials that can be verified so that they can believe you. You need to market your work in your community because they already trust you. Selling to strangers is harder because they don't know you and cannot substantiate if you are genuine or not.

4. Update your Course Often

Things change every day and so is what is in your course. You need to do frequent research to improve your content, adding what you think people may want to know and removing what is already obsolete. Keep going through the links in your course to see if they are still working. You never know if the website you were referring to remove the content or stopped existing altogether. These small details are what separates you from bad reviews.

5. Collect Feedback

If you are a genuine seller, you will want to follow up with your students to see if they got anything from your work. If they had any problems, it's important to know so that you can solve them in the future. Take their experiences so that you can use them for your testimonials in the future.

6. You can Create more Content Through the Steps Outlined Above

Advantages of Passive Income for Artists

1. People get to recognize your work because of the online platform. Gone are the days that artists needed to physically display their work. You even have a greater audience through marketing yourself online as opposed to physical spaces. This means you can make more money.

2. You get to learn from other people in the same field. People doing the same thing get to meet each other and discuss their methods of earning passive income from their art.

3. You get to travel the world and still make more art despite where you are. You can communicate with people you are teaching online which is always a plus. No one cares where you are as long as you deliver your product to your subscribers.

Conclusion

Passive income is not a get rich quick scheme as statistics have shown that most working people rely on their active incomes. That can be wrong because anything can happen, and they lose their jobs. That would mean that they won't have anything to fall back on which is very dangerous. One should strive to have most of their income passively maybe at least 95%. Passive income is not just for the rich but for anyone that is willing to learn and try new things. Be a little adventurous with your money and time to make a little extra money.

Every method of making passive income requires some know-how and a person that chooses it should invest some time to understand how it works to minimize risks. Of course, there are risks involved with making some of the investments, but with a good professional, you can get all the help you need. Many of the investments are available online and to everyone. That means you have no excuse as o why you are not using your resources to make passive income.

The fact that you can make money from your passions and talents is great because you require very little for you to take it to the next level. People in the world are all connected by the internet, that means that there is someone somewhere looking for that special something only you can do. Your skills can benefit someone somewhere even if you do not think so. Research is the pillar of making passive income. When in doubt, you can always search through the internet to see what other people with similar interests are doing.

Hard work is very valuable for people that want to make a living with passive income. Some people have been able to retire early because they have made enough money and keep making it as they travel the world. This is because they realize that one must work harder at the beginning so that money can keep flowing later. They do their homework first so that they can enjoy later. Remember that passive income requires patience before you see a return on your investment; therefore, don't give up even when it takes longer than other people. Your journey is different, and maybe you may have to change your method a little bit.

It is important to connect with people as you start this journey. You may need mentors that will show you the ropes of the industry. Take notes and learn from them. You will need a community of people that work in the same industry so that you can exchange notes and help each other when you are stuck. You also need to create a tribe of people that believe in you and will support your venture financially. These are the most important because they are the reason you will keep thriving. They will buy and recommend their friends to buy. These are the people you must keep happy and engaged at all times. You should genuinely care about them and give them what they want at all times.

As I said earlier, the methods here are not exhaustive. There are many more ways to make passive income than I could fit on this single volume. Keep learning about more ways, and even if you pick one of the ways I have shown you, you can keep improving on till you become a true master that other people can study. Don't be selfish. If you are good at a method of passive income, there are people somewhere that are struggling that could need your help. Offer courses to earn more passive income or offer free training as your way to give back to others.

Bonus Material: Earning – An Introduction To Earning With The Double Your Income Sequence

SECTION 1: THE SECRET OF FORMING MONEY HABITS (AND HOW TO ENFORCE THEM)

You are a collection of your favorite habits.

And, you have a niche set of habits that contribute to the money you can earn and keep, during your average month. Understanding the science behind these habits will help you positively influence the energy you spend on making more money.

A habit is a practice that you have used so often, that it has become an internalized, autonomic blueprint – a kind of default program for how to execute a specific action.[1]

Habits become damaging when they stop being beneficial, and instead, become uncontrollable, unintentional and contrary to your personal goals. Most individuals carry with them the burden of many bad habits, which inadvertently keeps them from forging ahead and achieving their income goals.

According to Charles Duhigg, the reason why we struggle with habits is that they are as unique as we are. There is no quick-fix formula.

---

[1] Habit, Wikipedia, https://en.wikipedia.org/wiki/Habit

In order to effectively change your habits, you need enlightenment on a better process, and, on your stuck behavior. Then you can change your *cue-routine-reward* cycle.[2]

Cue: a trigger that puts your brain in automatic mode and chooses your habit

Routine: A physical, mental or emotional set of actions

Reward: What you gain from executing the habit

With fresh ideas and an understanding of how to break bad habit loops, you will adopt powerful new habits that will help you double your income every, single, month.

SECTION 2: HOW TO CREATE NEW MONEY HABITS

New habits are how you will double your income.

This means you need to:

#1: Identify and break bad habits, to free up room for fresh practices

[2] Duhigg, Charles, How Habits Work, https://charlesduhigg.com/how-habits-work/

#2: Identity and consciously adopt new habits, until they become automatic

This guide is not about the first step. If you want to learn how to break bad habits, I suggest reading Charles Duhigg's classic, "The Power of Habit."

What you do need to realize, is that a number of your existing habits need to change, to make room for the ones outlined in this guide. You must become consciously aware of your *cue-routine-reward cycle*, and interrupt it to stay on track.

You can do this effectively by replacing your existing rewards, with your new goal to double your income. To create a new habit, follow this simple process.

- **Identify the bad habit that must be replaced**
    - Waking up at 7 am to be at work at 8 am
- **Identify the harm it's causing**
    - Rushing and feeling harassed and irritated when you get to work
- **Understand and replace the reward from your bad habit**
    - Instead of instant gratification from sleeping late, your mood will be elevated, and your energy levels will be high at work
- **Implement the new habit, motivated by a stronger overall reward**

- Practice waking up at 5 am, arriving at work at 7:30 and easing into your day, to stimulate the positive mindset required for success

According to modern studies, it takes roughly 66 days before a new behavior becomes automatic.[3]

SECTION 3: THE 14 HABITS THAT WILL DOUBLE YOUR INCOME

Here are the habits you need.

Habit 1: SLEEP (You're Not Doing It Right)

Bill Gates, the co-founder of Microsoft, sleeps for 7 hours every night and reads for 1 hour before bedtime.

With over a third of Americans not getting enough regular sleep, most people vastly underestimate the importance of quality shuteye in their lives.

Over or under-sleeping exposes you to increased risk for chronic conditions, mental distress, stroke and heart disease.[4] According to a 2018 Poll by The National Sleep Foundation, excellent sleepers feel more effective at getting things done the next day.[5]

---

[3] Lally, Phillippa, How are Habits Formed: Modelling Habit Formation in the Real World, https://onlinelibrary.wiley.com/doi/abs/10.1002/ejsp.674

[4] 1 in 3 Adults Don't Get Enough Sleep, https://www.cdc.gov/media/releases/2016/p0215-enough-sleep.html

[5] National Sleep Foundation's 2018 Sleep in America Poll Shows Americans Failing to Prioritize Sleep, https://sleepfoundation.org/media-center/press-release/2018-sleep-in-america-poll-shows

The first habit you need to adopt is simple – get high quality, regular sleep.

Set a time every evening to go to sleep and stick to it. You should be in bed an hour before, your phone off and all screens far away from you. Read for an hour. Then, go to sleep for 7.

Wake up promptly, 7 hours later. Not a minute more.

Sticking to this new habit promises you stronger immunity, the improved concentration at work and greater emotional stability overall. Consistency will ensure that your circadian rhythms function well, and you never have trouble with restless sleep or with falling asleep.[6]

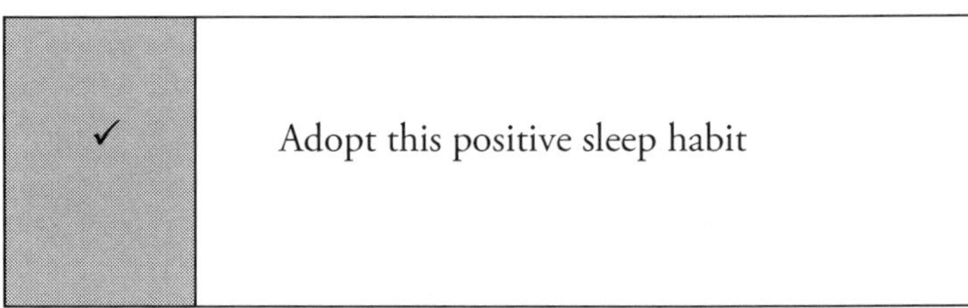

Habit 2: EXERCISE (It's Not Enough, or It's Too Much)

Ex-President Barack Obama works out for 45 minutes a day, six days a week. Thirty minutes or more of aerobic exercise is done daily by 76% of all successful people.[7]

---

[6] Mahabir, Nicole, How and Why Waking Up at the Same Time Every Day Can Improve Your Health, https://www.cbc.ca/life/wellness/how-and-why-waking-up-at-the-same-time-everyday-can-improve-your-health-1.4357391

[7] Cohen Jennifer, Exercise is One Thing Most Successful People Do Everyday, https://www.entrepreneur.com/article/276760

Aerobic exercise is the one consistent habit that will give you the energy you need to succeed. You should run, walk, jog, bike or take a class at the gym. Cardio gets your blood pumping, which is ideal for your brain and boosts your intelligence.[8]

The second habit you need to adopt – find and practice an aerobic exercise, daily.

Now, you need to pick 45 minutes to an hour, every day to get your cardio in. It makes no difference whether you do this in the morning, or late in the evening – as long as it is done every single day.

Consistency is how you will reap these many benefits.

Try to pick something that fits into your life, schedule and likes. You don't have to spend money, you simply have to get active. This means finding an exercise you will enjoy. Some people like boxing classes, others prefer to take a walk around the neighborhood.

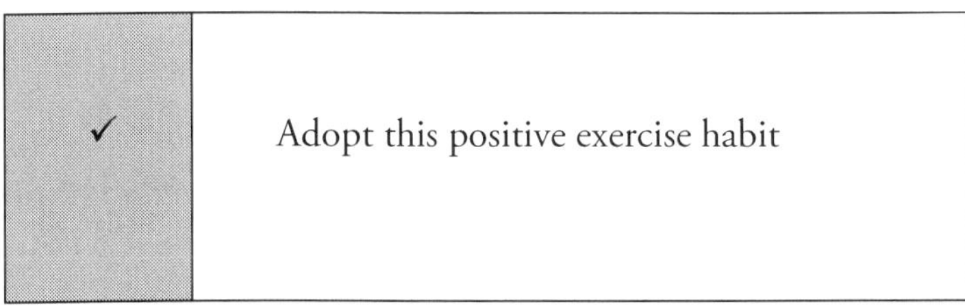

[8] Regular Exercise Releases Brain Chemicals Key for Memory, Concentration, and Mental Sharpness, From the May 2013 Harvard Men's Health Watch, https://www.health.harvard.edu/press_releases/regular-exercise-releases-brain-chemicals-key-for-memory-concentration-and-mental-sharpness

Habit 3: SOCIAL ENERGY (Here's One to Protect)

Oprah Winfrey, talk-show host, and owner of Harpo Studios meditates for 20 minutes every morning, shortly after waking up.

Meditation makes you more in-tune with yourself, how you feel, and how the world around you feels. It's great for focus, increased energy, decreased stress and lifts brain fog.[9]

The people around you have an impact on your energy levels. Successful people surround themselves with positive, go-getters – while the average person is drained by one or more toxic, or negative people in their lives. Social energy must be protected.

The third habit is – to meditate daily on how to optimize your social energy.

According to a Cigna Study, loneliness is at epidemic levels in America.[10] But this is never a good reason to allow anyone a place in your life.

Take a look at your connections and consider if they add, or take energy away from you as you meditate for 20 minutes every morning.

Extroverted, or introverted, you need the right kind of connections in your daily life. If you have energy vampires in your sphere, you must get rid of them to be at your best.

---

[9] Sun, Carolyn, I Tried This Oprah Meditation Hack Every Day for Two Weeks. Here Are My 5 Takeaways, https://www.entrepreneur.com/article/310039

[10] New Cigna Study Reveals Loneliness at Epidemic Levels in America, https://www.prnewswire.com/news-releases/new-cigna-study-reveals-loneliness-at-epidemic-levels-in-america-300639747.html

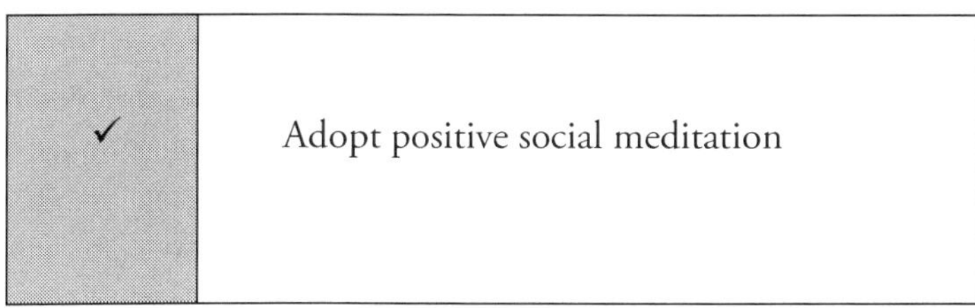

Habit 4: SELF-INVESTMENT (Knowing and Doing)

Albert Einstein believed in constant self-investment through learning, research and application of that newfound knowledge.

The day you stop learning, is the day you stop growing. And personal growth is what takes you towards income acceleration and success. Einstein knew that constant reading was critical to learning, but so was the application of the knowledge learned while reading.

He famously said that too much reading renders the brain lazy. To grow in his field, Einstein continued to study formally until he was 26, then pursued self-study. He was not, as many believe, a naturally talented genius savant – he studied, read and practiced knowledge.[11]

The fourth habit is – invest in your field of knowledge through reading and practice.

If you want to excel like Einstein, shift from consuming entertainment to consuming knowledge. This is easily done by dedicating an hour or more

[11] Shead, Mark, Are You Reading Too Much?, http://www.productivity501.com/are-you-reading-too-much/8874/

to reading and applying your newly discovered knowledge. Practice what you learn, to see the real difference.[12]

Carve an hour of your day, in the morning or evening to read a book and then realize its lessons. This can be split into 30 minutes of reading, 30 minutes of creating.

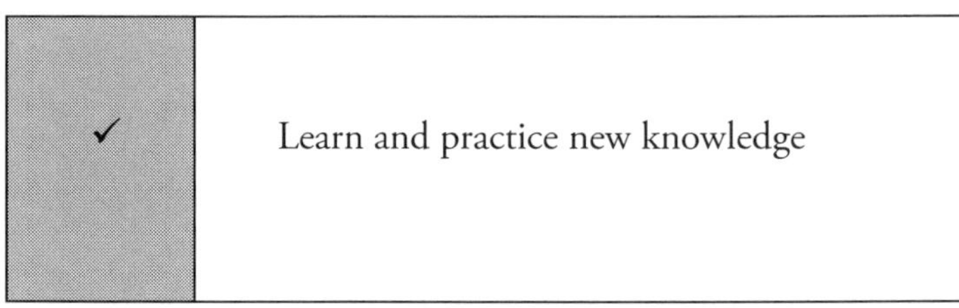

Habit 5: DELEGATION (Focus on The Big Picture)

Richard Branson, Founder of Virgin and hundreds of other companies, is famous for his practice of 'letting go, to grow.' He delegates to focus on the big picture.[13]

Delegation is a habit that most people fail to practice. Instead, they try to do everything themselves and end up burned out, exhausted and depleted.

---

[12] How Much Did Albert Einstein Study?, https://www.forbes.com/sites/quora/2017/12/28/how-much-did-albert-einstein-study/#1595adeb28bc

[13] Richard Branson: Why Delegation is Crucial for Success, https://www.virgin.com/entrepreneur/richard-branson-why-delegation-crucial-success

When you actively practice delegation, you become a talented multitasker, able to orchestrate and design your own career. It is at this point your income will inflate.

The fifth habit is – to practice delegation often and keep your eyes on the big picture.

Your career, or income goals, maybe the big picture for now. Knowing where you want to end up gives you clarity of purpose, and will help you assign what is not important to those around you. This must be done in all aspects of your life that consume your time.

This habit will kick in when someone makes demands on your time. Ask yourself if it contributes to your big picture. If it does not, find a creative way of delegating it to another human being. Make this a habit, and soon you will be surrounded by competent people.[14]

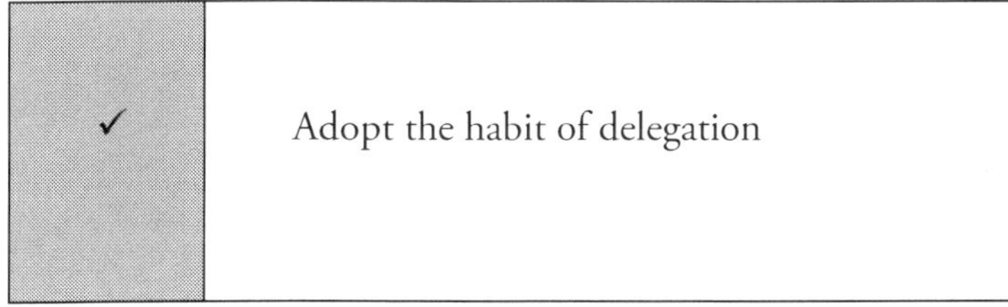

[14] Coleman, Alison, Delegate Like Branson: Hire People Who are More Talented Than You, https://www.forbes.com/sites/alisoncoleman/2015/01/25/delegate-like-branson-hire-people-who-are-more-talented-than-you/#4ce10d27cb3d

Habit 6: MENTORING (Learning and Teaching)

Marie Forleo is a life coach, philanthropist and entrepreneur, who believes in the power of mentoring and being mentored, to become hugely successful.[15]

In fact, she uses connections to grow her business at every level. With storytelling and the ability to build a community around her lifestyle brand, she was named Oprah's *"thought leader for the next generation."*

Your ability to surround yourself with the right people will be the single most useful habit you can adopt. Most people never actively practice the art of conscious mentoring.

The sixth habit is – to practice attracting network connections that will help you excel!

Who do you know that could teach you something important? Have you ever met someone who you wanted to learn from? Teaching and learning is fundamental to networking, and the basis for all positive relationships, in a corporate environment.[16]

Every day, you should consciously invest more energy in stimulating and improving mentor relationships that will help you grow and succeed as a person in your field. Be ruthlessly selective about your friends and who you spend the most time with.

---

[15] Brouwer, Allen, Lavery, Cathryn, Why Marie Forleo Says This One Marketing Trick Is So Important, https://www.entrepreneur.com/article/305586

[16] Forleo, Marie, Networking For Introverts W/Susan Cain, https://www.marieforleo.com/2013/11/susan-cain-introverts-networking/

Allow others to mentor you, and be mentored by you, in a working environment.

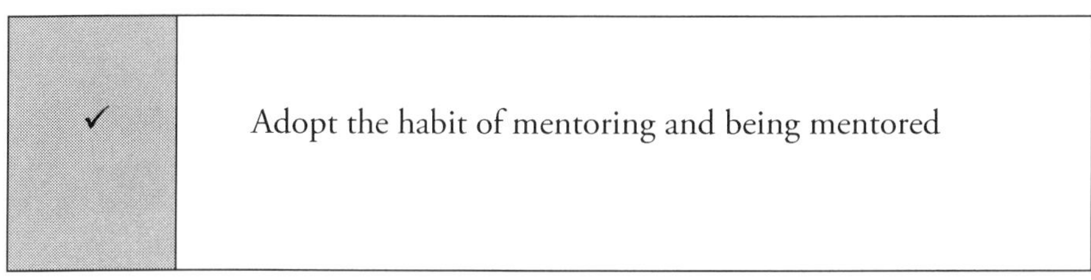

Habit 7: YOUR 96 MINUTES (This is Your Most Valuable Time)

Stephen King is known for his work ethic and ability to produce six good pages of writing every day consistently. He does this by following the same productivity routine daily. [17]

You need to have the discipline and consistency required, to do something for your direct productivity benefit, for 96 minutes a day. Why 96 minutes?

Science says that everyone has 96 highly productive minutes every day, a time window when you have the most energy and are at your best. If you harness this power and use it for your ultimate goal of earning more money, it shifts from possible, to probable.[18]

[17] Cotterill, Thomas, Stephen Kings Work Habits, https://thomascotterill.wordpress.com/2012/09/13/stephen-kings-work-habits/

[18] The Rule of 96 Minutes to Productivity, http://sapience.net/blog/the-rule-of-96-minutes-to-productivity/

The seventh habit is – Spend 96 minutes a day working on your main career goal.

Discover when your 96 minutes kicks in. It might be just after waking up. It might be late at night when everyone else is sleeping. Find your window and use it.

Spend those 96 minutes focused exclusively on your main career goal. If that is to get a promotion, this is when you will plan and execute a strategy. If it is to launch a website, this is when you will put in the work.

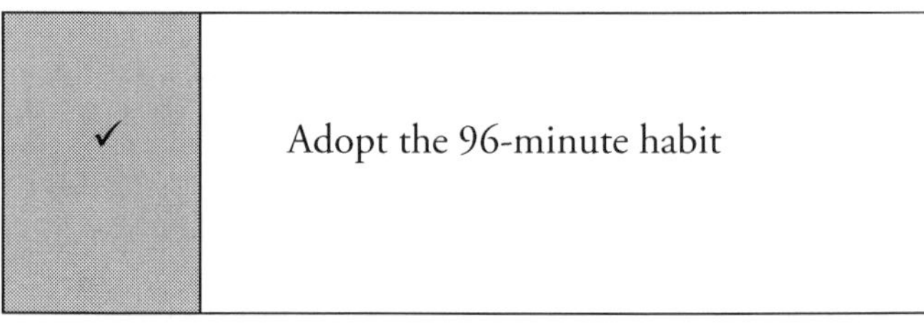

✓	Adopt the 96-minute habit

Habit 8: INNOVATION (Get to The Core of Things)

Elon Musk, the founder of PayPal, SpaceX and Tesla, is a known innovator and practices the Richard Feynman technique mixed with first principles, to stay creative. [19]

The underlying concept of this technique is to not try and remember, but to understand – because when you do, you automatically remember. It's a way to entertain new ideas and be creative in a way that promotes productivity.

[19] The Feynman Technique: The Best Way to Learn Anything, https://fs.blog/2012/04/learn-anything-faster-with-the-feynman-technique/

Knowledge to Elon, is about understanding the fundamental principles of a thing, to know the trunk and branches before diving headlong into the details, or the leaves of an idea.

The eighth habit is – when learning something new, to understand its core first.

Applying this to your career will make you a forward-thinking innovator. For example, if you are a psychologist, you would benefit from learning more about neuroscience, because it is at the core of your field. Competency is all about strong, unshakable fundamentals.[20]

Spend 30 minutes every day learning something that reinforces how you innovate in your chosen field. Soon you will be questioning, brainstorming and seeing patterns that may amount to improvements you can implement.

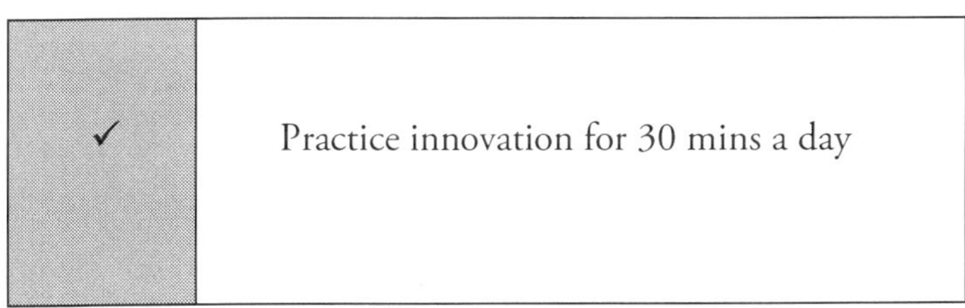

Habit 9: THE WIN-WIN (Mutually Beneficial Relationships)

Stephen Covey, author of the smash hit "The 7 Habits of Highly Effective People" advocated the importance of win-win relationships.

---

[20] Stillman, Jessica, 3 Smart Strategies Genuises Like Albert Einstein and Elon Musk Use to Learn Anything Faster, http://www.businessinsider.com/3-strategies-geniuses-like-elon-musk-use-to-learn-anything-faster-2017-10?IR=T

According to Covey, most people approach life with a scarcity mindset, as opposed to an abundance mindset. Because of this, social interactions become unbalanced.[21]

There are several types of human interaction, win-lose, lose-lose, lose-win – but none are as powerful or effective as the win-win. When you practice win-win interactions, your engagements are mutually beneficial, and people will enjoy working with you.

The ninth habit is – to practice win-win human interactions in your daily life.

When you do, you will find that people flock to you, because they see the benefits of doing business with you. When everyone benefits, you can succeed together.

This habit will cue when someone asks you for something. This should be your trigger to think about how you can make the interaction a win-win scenario. Covey says, to take consideration and courage into account, and to be creative in your problem-solving.

As you create win-win results, your influence will grow in your field. Remember that there is enough success around for everyone, and you can create it for them!

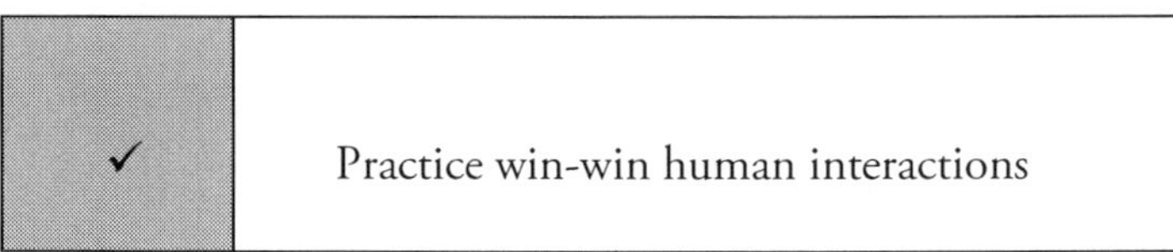

[21] Hussain, Anum, 7 Habits of Highly Effective People [Book Summary], https://blog.hubspot.com/sales/habits-of-highly-effective-people-summary

Habit 10: SPEAK UP (Know and Communicate Your Value)

Tyra Banks, ex-supermodel, TV producer and personality, based her career success on the ability to speak up, negotiate and get what she desires most.

She made a habit of speaking clearly, frankly and openly about her value with the people around her. Too often, we get stuck in the habit of remaining passive, and silent about our worth. Promotions and opportunities will pass you by because you failed to speak up.

The tenth habit is – to speak up when necessary about your value as an employee.

Tyra explains, that it is a shift from an 'I need' to an 'I deserve' mindset. Instead of explaining to your employer why you need a raise, you should explain why you deserve one. This is easily done by focusing on your value – or how you positively contribute to the company.[22]

This is another habit that will cue when you identify opportunities or feel that you deserve a promotion at your job. In meetings, be open about your contributions to the success of projects or initiatives. Speak up about how you, as a person, make things better.

Getting into the habit of communicating your worth to people around you, positions you for rapid advancement. If you cannot see and communicate your value, the higher-ups will not see it either. Be persistent. Have a clear voice. And do not get lost in the crowd.

---

[22] Atalla, Jen, Tyra Banks on How to Ask for a Raise, http://www.businessinsider.com/tyra-banks-how-to-ask-for-a-raise-2018-4?IR=T

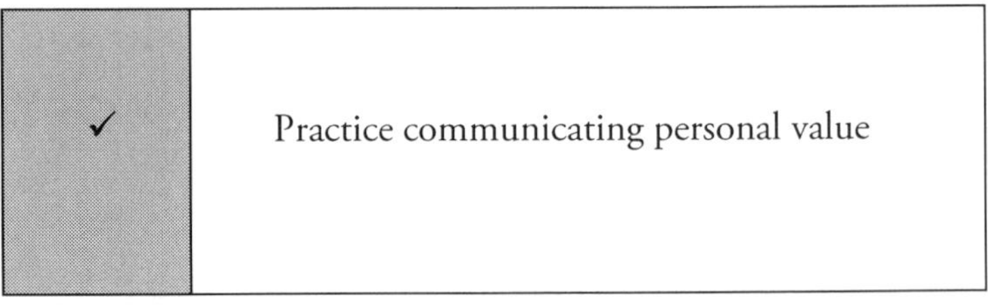

✓	Practice communicating personal value

Habit 11: PAY YOURSELF FIRST (This is Ground-breaking Advice)

George Clason was the author who wrote the classic 'The Richest Man in Babylon' and taught people to pay themselves first, in order to gain real wealth.[23]

Imagine if, since you had started working at age 21, you had put away 10% of every paycheck. This is what it means to pay yourself first. Money saved and kept earns compound interest and grows exponentially over long periods of time.

People that want to be wealthy use this strategy to move from employed earning to investing. Investing money is how you break out of your income bracket altogether.

The eleventh habit is – to put 10% of every paycheck aside to grow your wealth.

It might seem like very little at first, but 5 years of putting away just $100.00, frees up $6000.00 for investment. It gives you options to supplement your salary as you age.

---

[23] Canfield, Jack, The Key to Wealth: Pay Yourself First, http://jackcanfield.com/blog/the-key-to-wealth-pay-yourself-first/

To start the habit, every time you are paid – immediately take 10% of that total amount and put it in a separate account. You cannot touch this money. It is there simply to exist and earn you money from long-term growth.

The pay yourself first habit will help you clear away your debt, and get you investing at a young age. Get into this habit early, and you will benefit from time itself.

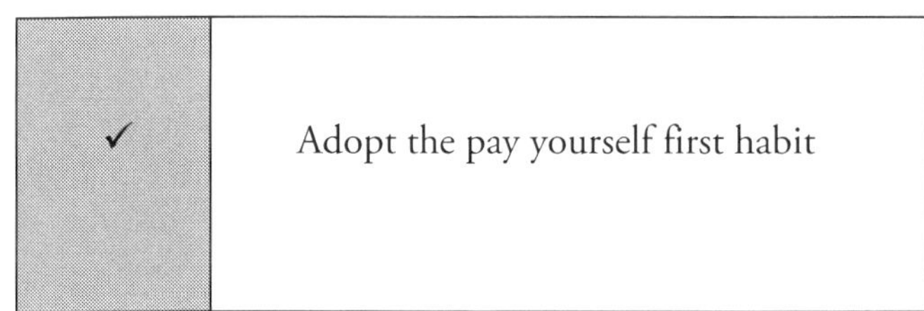

Habit 12: SIDE HUSTLE (Spend Your Time for Returns)

Rob Kalin never meant Etsy.com to be such a smash success. Initially, it was simply his side hustle, born from a desire to make wood-encased computers. [24]

Rob Kalin is a furniture designer who started Etsy as a place to sell his wares. It was a side hustle, an increasingly common play among

[24] Green, Penelope, Scratching an Itch, https://www.nytimes.com/2016/05/05/style/etsy-rob-kalin.html

Millennials. Some 61% of Millennials work on their side hustles once a week or more.[25]

This is usually a job that earns them money beyond their 9-5, or a personal project with income potential that they are developing. What is your side hustle?

The twelfth habit is – work on your side hustle twice a week.

On Mondays and Thursdays, or Tuesdays and Fridays you should dedicate a couple of hours to your side hustle. This is a second business, born from your creative or analytical talents that may become a solid earner for you down the line.

Scheduling in time to develop your secondary projects is important for personal growth, and increasing your income. Many Millennials discover that once their side businesses reach a certain level, they can either sell them or commit fulltime to their passions.

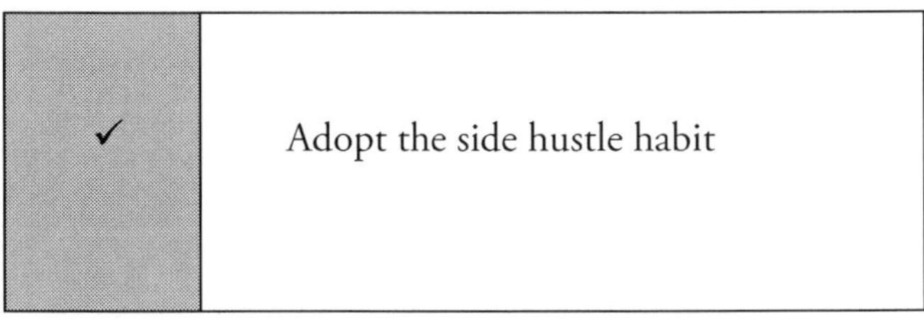

[25] Sophy, Joshua, More Than 1 in 4 Millennials Work a Side Hustle, https://smallbiztrends.com/2017/07/millennial-side-hustle-statistics.html

Habit 13: SUNDAY REVIEW (3 Hours to Financial Freedom!)

Suze Orman, a personal finance expert and personality, is known for teaching people to pick just one thing about their finances to work on, at a time. [26]

She called it the 'one and done' method, and it simplifies the huge challenge of getting hold of your financial situation. Many people find their finances overwhelming, and so never take proactive steps towards understanding and controlling them.

The thirteenth habit is – to spend 3 hours every Sunday focusing on one financial problem.

You might need to save, or clear debt, or better understand your expenses and how to curb them. Whatever you need, you will tackle it during a designated time, every Sunday.

When you practice the habit of reviewing your finances regularly, to better understand and control them, you will change your life.

Make sure that you pick only one simple thing at a time so that you can properly digest and institute changes as necessary. Spend the time learning and streamlining for your ultimate benefit, as a responsible financial planner.

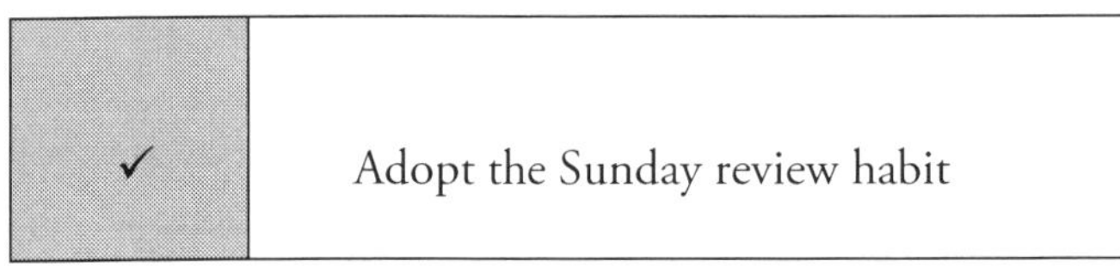

✓	Adopt the Sunday review habit

[26] Financial Resolutions for 2017? Just Do This One Thing, https://www.suzeorman.com/blog/financial-resolutions-for-2017-just-do-this-one-thing

Habit 14: MINIMALISM (Know How to Spend)

Steve Jobs, Founder of Apple, was a noted minimalist and wore the same black turtleneck every day for many, many years.

Popularized by Silicon Valley, minimalism reduces decision-fatigue, a common problem in today's overcrowded, ultra-informed society. With so much information and choice out there, it is no wonder you struggle to make good decisions for yourself.[27]

The theory goes that you can only make so many strong decisions in a day. The minimalist habit, allows you to dedicate those decisions to things that matter, like spending for value.

The fourteenth habit is – to spend with minimalism in mind.

Consumer culture is not for the truly rich. Instead, these individuals spend more money on a single item of quality, than repeated spending on numerous low-quality items.

Get into the habit of spending money on quality items, instead of cheaper items that will wear and degrade. This will free up your time as you make fewer wardrobe decisions. Instead of spending your creative energy there, you will spend it at work, where it matters most.

Less items of higher quality will simplify and improve your life.

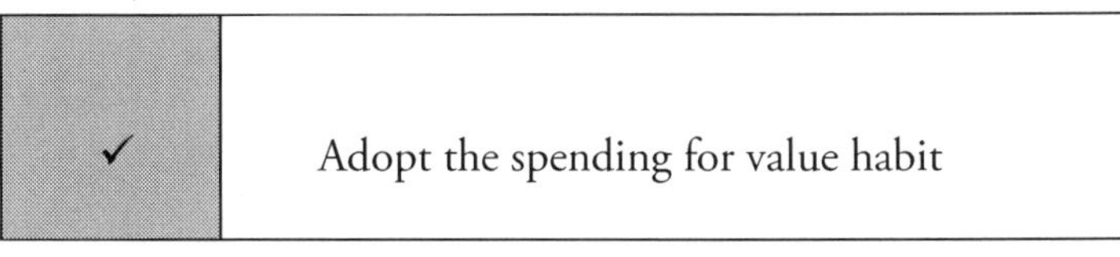

[27] Steve Jobs and Minimalism, http://www.applegazette.com/ipod/steve-jobs-and-minimalism/

SECTION 4: THE GOLDEN RULE OF SUCCESS SEQUENCING

Your habits determine your behavior, but one thing is more important.

Focus.

Your attention is a form of currency that will either enrich or impoverish your life. That is why they call it 'paying attention.' Focus is the literal gateway to learning, reasoning, decision-making, problem-solving and perception.[28]

That is why consistent focus on your habits is the golden rule of success.

None of the people you have read about in this guide could have succeeded without an all-encompassing focus on their daily habits. Every individual here keeps a rigorous, personalized schedule that optimizes these habits.

Success, like your daily habits, is incredibly personal. Only you can decide when you have achieved a high enough level of success. And your habits are the stepping stones!

If you want to double your income, nothing is keeping you from it, but your habits. When you remove the bad and replace it with these powerful income-generating habits, you will immediately experience rapid change that will reshape your life.

---

[28] Dr Taylor, Jim, Focus is The Gateway to Business Success, https://www.huffingtonpost.com/dr-jim-taylor/focus-is-the-gateway-to-b_b_4206552.html

That is why your primary focus must be a habitual practice, according to a personalized schedule. Without it, expect to fall back into bad patterns of behavior.

SECTION 5: THESE HABITS WILL MATTER MOST!

According to a study from Northwestern University, a domino effect happens when you adopt one lasting good habit.[29]

In other words, exercising every day will encourage positive eating habits. In turn, this may spread to you getting better quality sleep and performing better at work. Management of these small, seemingly insignificant habits starts with internalizing just one.

I want you to pick a habit from this list to act as your linchpin habit.

Then I want you to dedicate the next 66 days to internalizing that habit, and when you feel capable, adopt more from this list.

Even if you struggle to adopt more of these habits, I want you to commit to just the one. At no point over the next 66 days will you, at any point, stop practicing that habit.

The first couple in this list have the most impact. They directly affect your daily performance. This is how you will naturally double your income in the short term.

[29] Clear, James, How to Create a Chain Reaction of Good Habits, https://jamesclear.com/domino-effect

Consider the domino effect active in you right now. But it is focused on negative habits. Switch to replacing them with positive habits, and you will soar!

The habits that matter most are the ones you learn to keep. Make them part of who you are, and soon you will leap an income bracket.

SECTION 6: WILLPOWER OR WONTPOWER: YOU DECIDE

The number 1 barrier to change is a mysterious thing called 'willpower.'

Those who have it are strong. Those who lack willpower are weak.

That is what we are taught to believe in our modern society. Your ability to resist short-term temptations is chalked up to your measure of willpower.

But you are never told what it is, or how to get it. How is it meant to take over, when you have no idea how it works?

Now I am going to lift the veil.

Willpower is little more than self-control. It is the conscious act of choosing what is right, over what is easy. It is picking cognition, over emotion. It is discipline.[30]

Willpower is a *habit.*

---

[30] What You Need to Know About Willpower: The Psychological Science of Self-Control, http://www.apa.org/helpcenter/willpower.aspx

Right now, you habitually give in to your desires. What you need to do is replace this with your long-term plan for success. Say no to instant gratification!

Practice consciously choosing to focus on what is most important, every day.

If you don't want to exercise, use your willpower. Emotions drive your thoughts. Replace them with conscious thoughts that are more beneficial. You must exercise, to feel good today, tomorrow, this week. You must exercise to earn more and be better.

Practice willpower as a habit, and soon it will take over.

SECTION 7: REGAINING YOUR FAITH IN FREE WILL

'But I have so much to do.'

'I'll begin after my major project is over.'

'I'll just let this week pass, and I'll be ready.'

It is human nature to wait for the ideal time to change. You might have bought this guide with the intent to adopt these habits 'at some point.'

This is because you have lost faith in free will. Free will is your ability to choose between different courses of action, unimpeded. Now, life is all about impediments, but that does not mean you cannot choose to be better. You can.

We are all made up of a unique blend of strengths, weaknesses, circumstances and perceptions. Your free will must be exercised in accordance with your make-up, within your unique context, under your special circumstances.

The price of freedom is struggling.

The price of earning more is learning to be better.[31]

Then being better – every day!

If you cannot be better consistently, hope is lost.

In this way, free will gives you the opportunity to be whoever you want, as long as you are willing to go through the wringer to get there. It will be hard! If it were easy, everyone would be successful and living these rare lives.

My advice to be something is to practice.

Start and start *today*.

---

[31] Dr Schwartz, Seth, Do We Have Free Will, https://www.psychologytoday.com/us/blog/proceed-your-own-risk/201311/do-we-have-free-will

Check Out Our Other AMAZING Titles:

1. Resolving Anxiety and Panic Attacks

A Guide to Overcoming Severe Anxiety, Controlling Panic Attacks and Reclaiming Your Life Again

Worldwide, one in six people is affected by a mental health disorder. So you are not alone in this (Ritchie & Roser, 2019). There is a difference between clinical anxiety and everyday anxiety. Everyday anxiety is normal and in often cases, it is necessary, while chronic anxiety will leave you functionally impaired. This book will not only inform you about anxiety and panic attacks but also introduce you to various methods and techniques that aid in getting rid of anxiety. It is a perfect package if you want to make long-lasting, meaningful changes in your life in a way that gets rid of anxiety. Knowledge is power, so gaining information about anxiety and panic attacks already puts you in the lead against them.

In the first chapter, we'll start with the basic knowledge of panic attacks and anxiety. The symptoms of both are pretty much the same, but there are some major differences as well. Knowing their difference and similarities can help you clearly understand your condition. Some basic ways of coping with them are also explained alongside their symptoms.

After gaining knowledge about anxiety and panic attacks in the first section, you will seek answers and ways to overcome them. The second chapter goes more in detail about the physical effects of anxiety. There are some types of anxiety which are also talked briefly about in the chapter. There are also therapies and treatments that are used to overcome and control anxiety. Their details are discussed in the chapter from where you can figure out what sort of treatment will suit you better. Some other ways of coping with anxiety are also discussed and they will surely prove beneficial to the reader.

The third chapter will make you aware of how interrelated physical and mental healths are. There are also details on how to improve one's physical health to influence a person's anxiety positively. You will also learn how important practicing well-being is. If you are to ignore physical health, it will cause problems for your mental health as well.

The fourth chapter will delve deep into mindfulness and its vast benefits. Mindfulness is a very powerful tool we have but don't know how to use. It can be practiced through meditation techniques, etc. It makes us see things more clearly than ever before. Practicing Mindfulness will arm you against any anxiety and panic attacks. In this chapter, it is explained in detail what it means and what are its advantages.

In the fifth chapter, we will learn about meditation and how can it help manage anxiety. We first start off by knowing what it is. You also have got to know its benefits and various techniques from which one can pick according to their choice. We will also learn the accurate posture you should have during meditation. We will learn how mediation reinforces our brain to stave off anxiety and panic attacks. It is a long road but a successful one for sure. Besides helping us out with anxiety and panic disorder, meditation has numerous other benefits for our body and mind.

The sixth chapter will explore the meaning behind self-love and its importance in fighting anxiety. Our battle with anxiety has to start from a positive ground. We first have to be fully comfortable and respectful towards ourselves. You will also find out how lack of self-love can actually breed anxiety.

Opening about anxiety is not an easy task but could be very helpful against anxiety. How to go about the whole process is talked about in detail in the seventh chapter. You will also learn how to evaluate your therapist and choose the right one. In this chapter, there are also guidelines for people who have just recently become aware of their anxiety and now they want to seek help. It will give them knowledge about things to consider when talking to someone about mental health, what you should accept and be prepared for. There is also information about talk therapy there.

In the eighth chapter, we address the misunderstanding about anxiety. Despite affecting so many people, it remains a different experience for all of them. There are also common mistakes pointed out in that chapter which we'll go into detail the mistakes that make our anxiety worse.

The ninth chapter is about where we talk about putting our foot down and start to incorporate practices into our life which will help you get rid of anxiety and panic attacks. We will learn how to manage our responses. It is basically a comprehensive listing of all the things you should be avoiding or adapting to lead a healthy lifestyle free of anxiety.

2. Cognitive Behavioral Therapy

How CBT Can Be Used to Rewire Your Brain, Stop Anxiety, and Overcome Depression

Cognitive stems from cognition, which encapsulates the idea of how we learn and the knowledge that we carry. The things you learn are part of your cognition, and what you do with that information is included in that category as well. Cognition includes a wide list of information that you might not fully realize.

Behavior is what we do. It is how we act. The things that you choose to say to other people are all about your behavior. How you react to what others have to say will exhibit your behavior as well. Your behavior is all about your mind interacting with your body and how that interacts with the people and other things that surround you.

Therapy is any form of help, usually from a trained professional, to help improve on whatever the therapy is specified for. You might get physical therapy to help regain strength in your knee after having a serious surgery. You can also get therapy to help overcome an alcohol or drug addiction.

Throughout this book, we're going to give you the basis you need to start understanding cognitive behavioral therapy. The three together—cognitive, behavioral, therapy—all make up CBT, which is a method that is going to directly help you overcome the mental illness that you are hoping to treat.

Therapy can be expensive, and even if you do have the means to go through with this process, you might struggle to find the right therapist. Sometimes, you might live in an area where there is only one therapist within a close distance, but you don't have a vibe with them that you find to be helpful. You might also find that you are desperate for help and that you want a therapist, but insurance coverage isn't always good for this.

By reading this book, you'll be able to find the tools you need to help with overcoming your most challenging thoughts. We are going to take you through the steps to identify the root issues and come up with specific methods to get you through.

Want to read more? Purchase our book on ***Cognitive Behavioral Therapy*** *today!*

3. Effective Guide On How to Sleep Well Everyday

The Easy Method For Better Sleep, Insomnia And Chronic Sleep Problems

"A well spent day brings happy sleep." — Leonardo da Vinci

Are you experiencing the worst restless feeling? Has your doctor diagnosed you with insomnia, restlessness, sleeplessness? When the whole world around you seems to be in peaceful deep slumber, you are the one who is restless. No matter what term is used to describe it, the fact is that it is you who is actually going through insomnia, and nothing could feel worse than that.

So you drag yourself from bed in the morning feeling as earth, with its entire lock stock and barrel, has decided to perch on your head for the day. Yet you go through the motions of the day, though you barely manage to make it through the hours. By the early night, you fall on to bed hoping this night will be different because you're dead tired and nothing will keep you from sleeping like a log. It's 2.00 a.m. now, dawn is breaking through and there you are, still wide awake and ready to scream to the world because no matter how tired you are or how hard you have tried, you simply can't get to sleep.

While there are proven facts and evidence of the devastating effects of sleeping less, the investigations are still on to establish the exact nature of effects resulting from too much sleep. Some researchers argue that people who sleep much longer than necessarily have a higher death rate. Physical and mental conditions such as depression or socioeconomic status can also lead to excessive sleep. There are other researchers who argue that the human body will naturally restrain it from sleeping more hours than really necessary. However, with research still underway for concrete evidence of the effects of over sleeping the best path you can choose is to adopt a sleeping pattern somewhere in the middle. According to the National Sleep Foundation, this middle range falls between seven and eight hours of sleep during the night. Despite these statistics, the best way to ensure you receive sufficient sleeping time is to let your own body act as your guide. You can always sleep a little extra if you feel exhausted or sleep a little less than usual if you feel you are oversleeping.

Dangers of Sleep deprivation.

Though sleep is something the average human being takes for granted, it is also one of the greatest mysteries in life. Just like we still don't have all the answers to the quantum field or gravity, researchers are still exploring the reasons behind the 'whats' and 'whys' of sleep. However, one fact unchallenged about sleep is that a proper sleep is paramount for maintaining good health. The general guideline regarding the optimal amount of sleep for an adult range from six to eight hours! If you carry on with too little or too much of this general guideline you are exposing yourself to the risk of adverse health effects.

Though sleep is something that comes naturally to many people, the problems of sleep deprivation have today become a pressing problem with more and more people succumbing to chronic sleeping disorders. Unfortunately, a great number of these people do not even realize that lack of sleep or sleep deprivation is at the root of their manifold problems in life. Scientific research also points out that lack of sleep on a continuous scale can lead to severe repercussions on your health.

If you have been experiencing impaired sleep patterns for a longer period, you also face the risk of:

- Severely impairing your immunity strength
- Promoting the risk of tumor growth, as it has been scientifically established that a tumor can grow at least two to three times faster among animals subjected to severe sleeping dysfunctions within a laboratory setting.
- Creating a pre-diabetic condition in the body. Insomnia creates hunger, making you want to eat even when you have already had a meal. This situation can lead to problems of obesity in turn.
- Critically impairing memory. How many times during the day have you found it difficult to remember even the most mundane and repetitive events when you have had no more than 4 – 5 hours of sleep? Even a single night of impaired sleep plays havoc with our memory faculties, just think what it can do to your brain if you consistently lose sleep.

- Ruining your performance level both physically and mentally as your problem-solving abilities will not be working in peak order.
- Stomach ulcers
- Constipation, hemorrhoids
- Heart diseases
- Depression, lethargy and other mood disorders
- Daytime drowsiness
- Irritability
- Low energy
- Low mental clarity
- Reaction time slows down
- Lower productivity
- More accidents and mistakes
- Lower levels of growth hormone and testosterone

The growth hormone in the body which is vital for maintaining our looks, energy, and skin texture is produced by the pituitary gland. The specialty of this hormone production procedure is that it is only produced during the times of deep slumber or during intense workout sessions. In the absence of normal production of the growth hormone, our bodies will start on a premature aging process. According to research, people suffering from chronic insomnia are three times more susceptible to contract fatal diseases. When you lose sleep overnight, you cannot make up for it by sleeping more the next day. A night's lost sleep will be lost forever. More alarmingly if you continue to lose sleep regularly, they will create a cumulative negative effect that will disrupt your general health. All in all, sleeping deficiencies can effectively make your life miserable, as you already know.

How Much Sleep Do I Really Need?

This is a question that remains a mystery just like the questions of why and what makes us want to sleep. In response to a question of how many hours of sleep do we really need, an expert has answered that it is actually lot less than what we have been taught. On the other hand, though a good night's sleep is vital for good health, overdoing the sleeping can be equally bad for us. But if you sleep less and continue this for too long, the result will be confusion between body and brain signals, resulting in muddled thoughts, lethargic feelings, and overall lassitude. So, the question remains, how many hours of sleep do we really need? Is it essential to sleep the prescribed number of eight hours a day or is catching up a good sleep on a five to six-hour basis enough?

The eight hours of sleep theory is increasingly becoming unpractical in this fast-paced lifestyle. Actually, the recommendation of eight hours of sleep arises based on the idea that our ancestors had their beauty sleep between 8-9 hours in the past. In today's context, this concept is regarded more or less as a myth. In a study conducted by the Sleep Research Center, youngsters within the age group of 8 to 17 generally sleep for about nine hours during the night. However, in the case of adults, this theory is not applicable as a majority of them are sleepless and many of them thrive after a solid sleep varying between 5-7 hours.

A research conducted by the National Institute of Health has established that people who sleep soundly for nine hours a day or more are actually two times more vulnerable than those who sleep less in developing Parkinson's disease. A study report released by the Diabetes Care states that people claiming to sleep less than five hours or more than nine hours daily are the ones with the highest risk of attracting diabetes. In contrast, a large number of contemporary studies prove that people with sleeping patterns that do not exceed or fall beyond seven hours daily possess the highest survival rate. The persons who experience sleeping disorders and sleep less than 4.5 hours have the worst survival rate.

When ascertaining the correct number of hours you should sleep, the fact is that there is no magic number of hours. It will depend on a person to person basis as well as factors like age, activity, and performance level. For example, smaller children and teenagers require more sleep compared to adults. Your personal requirements will not be the same as your friend or colleague who is of the same age and gender as you. Because your sleep needs are unique and individual. According to the National Sleep Foundation, the difference of sleep requirements between two people of the same age, gender, and activity level is due to their basal sleep needs and sleep debt.

Your basal sleep need is the number of hours of sleep you typically need to engage in optimal performance levels. The sleep debt comprises of the accumulated number of hours of sleep you have lost as a result of poor sleeping habits, a recent sickness, social demands, environmental factors, etc. A healthy adult generally possesses a basal sleep need between seven and eight hours each night. If you have experienced sleeping difficulties and as a result accumulated a sleep debt you will find that your performance level is not up to its usual standard, even if you wake up after seven or eight hours of restful sleep. The symptoms will be most apparent during the times the circadian rhythm naturally alters like during mid-afternoon or overnight. One of the ways of easing out of an accumulated sleep debt situation is to get a few extra hours of sleep for a couple of nights until you regain your natural sleeping rhythm and vitality during the day.

Understand what Kind of a Sleeper Are You?

Sleep, dear reader, is the precious restorative that rights so many physical and mental wrongs. The elixir that transforms life and puts a spring in your step, a smile on your face, and the feeling that you can take care of everything that comes your way is sleep. Undervalued, ignored, and forgotten until you wake up to the realization that it's one of the essential foundations of daily wellbeing.

So what kind of a sleeper are you? There are many studies and descriptions of how we sleep but the common consensus settles for the following five simple categories:

1. Lively, healthy early risers!

These happy individuals usually get the sleep they need and rarely feel exhausted or fatigued. They are typically younger than the other groups, usually married or with a long-term partner, working full-time and definitely a morning person with no serious medical conditions.

2. Relaxed and retired seniors.

This is the oldest group in the survey with half of the sample being 65 or older. They sleep the most with an average of 7.3 hours per night compared to 6.8 across all groups. Sleep disorders are rare even though there is a significant proportion with at least one medical disorder.

3. Dozing drones.

These busy people are usually married/partnered and employed but they often work much longer than forty hours a week. Frequently working up to the hour when they go to bed, they get up early so they're always short of sleep and struggle to keep up with the daily pressures of life. Statistically, they'll feel tired or fatigued at least three days a week.

4. Galley slaves.

This group works the longest hours and often suffers from weight problems as well as an unhealthy reliance on caffeine to get through the day. Shift workers often fall into this group and there is also a marked tendency to be a night owl or evening person. They get the least amount of sleep and are more likely to take naps yet, surprisingly, this group often believes that, despite the state of their health, they are getting enough sleep.

5. Insomniacs.

Here is the largest proportion of night people and many of them quite rightly believe they have a sleep problem. About half of this group feel they get less sleep than they need and the same proportion admits to feeling tired, fatigued and lacking energy most of the time.

So, which of the five groups do you think you fit into?

If you're a happy member of Group One, your sleep should by definition be absolutely fine. Don't worry. We've got some really good ideas to share with you to keep you right on track and we'll even add some special extra features to your nightly rest routine to maximize the experience. If you're not in this group, our aim is to help you become a full-time member of the healthy, happy sleepers' association! Membership is for life.

Group Three represents too many tired, irritable, and generally inefficient individuals whose quality of life is impaired because they're too tired too often. Their work suffers because they rarely have sufficient rest to successfully assimilate the day's events. Their home life is degraded because work intrudes too often and they're just too tired to enjoy the pleasures and comfort of a life away from work. Feeling tired becomes their default position and they know they need to do something to give their minds and bodies the rest they deserve. Individuals in this group frequently suffer from long- term mental, physical and emotional stress.

The fourth group is rightly described as the night owls. They work the longest hours and, as we noted above, they typically work shifts. The health problems associated with this group include a marked tendency towards obesity as well as a range of inflammatory diseases. Despite the fact that these people rarely look or feel well, they seem to ignore the evidence and usually claim to get enough sleep, relying on sugary energy drinks and caffeine to keep them awake during waking hours. They take naps because their bodies can't function without additional sleep during the day. An objective analysis of their health would typically reveal a range of health and wellbeing issues.

Insomniacs are the dominant members of Group Five, people who don't get enough sleep, can't get to sleep, and who know they have a problem. Unfortunately, many insomniacs end up taking prescription medication to deal with their symptoms and we have to question the benefits of this solution in light of the many unpleasant side effects associated with long-term sleeping pill dependency. For insomniacs, life is a constant struggle because of the accumulative effects of long-term sleep deprivation.

Health issues abound, depression becomes a major risk, their ability to function normally is often impaired, and they lose sight of their potential to deal successfully with life's daily challenges. They sometimes refer to their condition as living in a nightmare world where they are constantly exhausted and simply cannot function. It's completely understandable that a doctor would prescribe sleeping drugs because the dangers of sleep deprivation can be acute.

Before we begin to examine the practicalities of sleep, we need to know how much sleep is appropriate for each of us as individuals. It's not surprising that different age groups have different sleep requirements.

For example, very young children and infants can sleep in total for around 14 - 15 hours a day. And if you've got teenagers, you might have guessed that adolescents usually need more sleep than adults. Teens can easily sleep between 8.5 to 9.5 hours a night.

It's widely understood that during the first trimester, pregnant women often find they need a lot more sleep than usual. The fact is that if you feel tired during the day, find yourself yawning or taking a nap, you're short on sleep. And this is the time for you to do something practical, realistic, and effective to take care of the problem.

There are many myths surrounding the condition known as OAS or Obstructive Sleep Apnea. It's estimated that around 18 million Americans suffer from the condition but the numbers could be much higher because many people don't report the condition to their doctors. This condition is far more than just loud snoring, although snoring can be a sign of sleep apnea.

People with this condition skip breathing 400 times during the night. The delay in breathing can last from ten to thirty seconds and is then followed by a loud snore as breathing suddenly resumes. The normal sleep cycle is interrupted and this can leave sufferers feeling tired and exhausted during the day. It is a serious condition, especially since it can lead to accidents at work, problems when driving, as well as increasing the risk of heart attacks and strokes. It can affect people of all ages, including children, but tends to affect people more after the age of forty.

Weight also plays a part and there is evidence that shedding excess pounds can improve the condition. Despite all the advice and overwhelming evidence, there are still surprising numbers of sleep apnea sufferers who continue to smoke. Smoking is a perfect way to increase the severity and risks of this debilitating condition.

If you've already trimmed your weight, quit smoking and tried sleeping on your side but still suffer from the condition, you need to see your doctor. There are many treatments available including a special mask that delivers constant air flow to keep the breathing passage open. Lifestyle choices can clearly make a positive difference, too.

Your body, your brain, your mind and your emotional functioning all rely on sufficient sleep to operate efficiently. If you don't get enough sleep, everything suffers. Research suggests that it's much harder than you might imagine to adapt having less sleep than your body needs. The sleep deficit has to be repaid at some point or we'll experience increasingly severe problems.

Simple techniques of preparing for bed

1. Try to get to bed early. The recharging of the body's adrenal system usually takes place between 11p.m. and 1a.m. in the morning. The gallbladder uses the same time to release the toxin build up in the body. If you happen to be awake when both these functions are taking place within your body, there is the possibility of the toxin backing up to the liver which can endanger your health very badly.

Sleeping late are byproducts of modern living styles. However, the human body was created in synchronization of nature and its activities. That is why before the advent of electricity people used to go to bed just after sundown and wake up with sunrise.

2. Don't alter your bedtimes haphazardly. Try to stick to a pattern where you go to bed and wake up at the same time. This should be done even on weekends. The continuous pattern will help your body to fit into a rhythm.

3. Maintain a soothing bedtime routine. This can change from person to person. You can use deep breathing exercises, meditation, use of aromatherapy, a gentle relaxing massage given by your partner, or even going through a complete and relaxing skin care routine. The secret is to get into a rhythm which makes you comfortable, relaxed, and ready for bed. Repeating it every day will help in easing out the tensions of the day.

4. Refrain from taking any heavy fluids two hours before bed time. This habit will minimize the number of times you need to visit the bathroom in the middle of the night. You should also make a habit of going to the bathroom just before you get into bed, so that you will not get the urge during night time.

5. Eat a meal enriched with proteins several hours before your bed time. The protein will enhance the production of L-tryptophan which is essential for the production of serotonin and melatonin. Follow up your meal with some fruit to help the tryptophan to cross easily across the blood brain barrier.

6. Refrain from taking any snacks while in bed or just before bed and reduce the level of sugar and grains in your dinner time as it will raise

the blood sugar level, delaying sleep. When the body starts metabolizing these elements and the blood sugar level start dropping you will find yourself suddenly awake and unable to go back to sleep.

7. A hot bath before bed is found to be very soothing. When the body temperature is stimulated to a raised level during late evening by the time you get into bed, it will be ready to drop, signaling slumber time to your brain.

8. Stop your work and put them away ideally one to two hours before bed. The interval between work and bedtime should be used for unwinding from the pressure and tension of work. It is essential that you approach your bed with a calm mind instead of being hyped up about some matter.

9. If you prefer reading, a novel with an uplifting story instead of a stimulating one like suspense or mystery is recommended. Or the suspense will keep you up half the night awake trying to visualize the end to the mystery!

A Few Lifestyle Suggestions to Make You Sleep Better

Don't take medications and drugs unless it is absolutely necessary for your health and wellbeing. A majority of prescribed and over the counter drugs can cause changes in your sleeping patterns.

Avoid drinks with alcohol or caffeine. Caffeine takes longer to metabolize in the body so that your body will experience its effects much longer after consumption. That is why even the cup of coffee you had in the evening will keep you awake during the night. Some of the medications and drugs in the market also contain caffeine which account for their capacity to generate sleeping irregularities. Though alcohol can make you feel drowsy the effect is very much short lived. Once the feeling goes away, you will find that sleep is eluding you for many hours and even the sleep that you finally reach will not take you to deep slumber after alcohol. In the absence of deep sleep, your body will not be able to perform its usual healing and regeneration process is vital for lasting healthiness.

Engage in regular exercise activities. If you are contained in an 8-hour office job, you should make sure that your body receives plenty of exercise which can dramatically increase your sleep health. The best time to exercise is, however, not closer to your bedtime but in the morning.

Keep away from sensitive food types that will keep you awake at night like sugar, pasteurized dairy foods, and grains. These foods can result in congestion, leading to gastric disorders.

The sleep apnea risk is enhanced amongst people with weight issues. If you think you have gained a few extra pounds and during this time you have also experienced sleeping trouble focus on losing the extra weight as a priority. The sleeping issue will correct automatically.

If your body is going through a hormone upheaval like during menopausal or premenopausal time, seek advice from your family physician, as this time can lead to sleeping difficulties.

Want to read more? Purchase our book on ***Effective Guide On How to Sleep Well Everyday*** *today!*

Made in the
USA
Columbia, SC

78758934R00079